For the Love of God:
The Epistles of John

JUSTO L. AND CATHERINE GUNSALUS GONZÁLEZ

Women's Division
The General Board of Global Ministries
The United Methodist Church

ISBN # 978-1-933663-40-1
Library of Congress Control Number: 2009937817

Printed in the United States of America

CONTENTS

PREFACE

There is no writing that we find more rewarding than Bible study and commentary, for it forces us to look at Scripture anew, to analyze the text, to consider its relevance and its challenges, and to seek ways to present all of this to our audience. Thus, when offered the opportunity to write this book we took the task with immediate enthusiasm. As we expected, writing it has been both challenging and rewarding.

There is, however, a danger in any such book. It is too easy to substitute its reading for careful study of the biblical text itself. When this happens, the book draws attention away from its very object, and rather than illumining Scripture it becomes one more layer between readers and the Bible itself. For this reason, we urge our readers to begin and end the study of each chapter in this book with a careful reading of the Epistles of John themselves, and to have the text at hand while reading what we have written. We hope that in so doing, the text will become clearer to you, and its call to faith, obedience, and love all the more persuasive and urgent. If so, as First John would say, "our joy will be complete"!

Justo L. González
Catherine Gunsalus González

INTRODUCTION

The Place of the Epistles of John
within the New Testament

The three Epistles of John are to be found toward the end of the New Testament, among those that are usually called "universal," "general," or "catholic" Epistles, because they appear to be letters written in general to the entire church, or at least to no one in particular—James; First and Second Peter; First, Second, and Third John; and Jude. However, as we shall see, one of the three Epistles of John is not universal in that sense, for it is addressed to a specific individual—Gaius. Thus the term "general" does not apply equally to all three, even though there is ample reason to keep them together, for there are many similarities and points of contact among them.

These three Epistles are also classified as part of one of three great bodies of literature in the New Testament. These are the Pauline corpus—Epistles by Paul and some of his disciples or companions; the Lukan corpus—The Gospel of Luke and Acts; and the Johannine corpus—the Gospel of John, the three Epistles we are studying, and Revelation.

Unity and Diversity of the Johannine Corpus

Traditionally it was thought that all of these books were written by the same person, and that this was the Apostle John, the son of Zebedee. But even from a very early time there were doubts about this. For instance, in the middle of the second century Papias of Hierapolis declared that the Epistles were not the work of the same author as that of the Gospel. Hierapolis, the city where Papias resided, is very close to Laodicea, one of the cities mentioned in the seven letters in the Book of Revelation, and Papias would therefore be acquainted with what was said in the area about John and his writings. Several centuries later Isho'dad of Merv declared that, although many thought that the Fourth Gospel and First John were written by the same person and that this was the Apostle John, it was obvious that the two could not have been the result of the same writer. Indeed, Isho'dad goes so far as to affirm that the Epistle is quite inferior to the Gospel in its theology and in its style, and that therefore it does not have the same apostolic authority as the Gospel of John. But such doubts about the Epistles' author and his connection with the Fourth Gospel and with Revelation slowly disappeared, and for centuries the Johannine authorship of the entire corpus was seldom questioned, so that medieval as well as reformation commentators took it for granted. It was only in the modern age, with the development of new methods of textual analysis and historical criticism, that doubt arose as to the single authorship of the entire body of literature attributed to John.

Even without denigrating First John, as Isho'dad did, it is clear that there are marked differences among the three portions of the Johannine corpus—the Gospel, the Epistles, and Revelation. First of all the Gospel and the Epistles, like the rest of the New Testament, quote the Old Testament from the Septuagint, which was the most commonly used Greek translation of the ancient Hebrew books. Revelation seems to be using an entirely different translation, without parallel elsewhere in early Christian literature. (One of us, Justo, has a different theory about this. He suspects that what

John of Patmos is doing in Revelation is translating from memory as he goes. Justo grew up speaking Spanish, and any Bible passages that he knows by heart he knows in Spanish. Quite often, when speaking in English, he finds himself translating in his mind what he knows in Spanish. Quite possibly this is the situation in Revelation, where John quotes Hebrew literature in practically every verse. He is simply translating in his mind as he goes.)

Then, the three parts of the corpus are quite different in their style. The contrast between Revelation and the other books is obvious even to a casual reader. The Gospel tells stories about Jesus, and then draws from them Christological affirmations—the well known "I am" sayings: "I am the way, the life, and the truth," "I am the resurrection and the life," "I am the bread of life," and many others. The Epistles do not tell such stories, and say little about the life of Jesus. Revelation, in clear contrast with the others, speaks in dramatic and cosmic images—the woman clothed in the sun, the dragon and the two beasts, the bowls of wrath, and many others. Furthermore, while there are Hebraisms present in the Gospel, there is no doubt that Revelation's use of Greek—the language in which the entire New Testament is written—is more stilted and awkward than that in the Gospel or the Epistles, which would seem to indicate that its author did not have the same facility in Greek.

Although in a moment we shall turn to some of the similarities linking these various elements of the Johannine corpus, there is a difference in theological emphasis that is worth noting. All three—the Gospel, the Epistles, and Revelation—are concerned with the present life of believers and their obedience to the will of God. But while Revelation draws on a vision of the future to call for present faithfulness and obedience, the Gospel and the Epistles look mostly to the past for guidance—to the life of Jesus and his teaching. Clearly, Revelation bases its exhortations and its visions on the life of Jesus, the Lamb who was slain, and there is a future expectation in both the Gospel and the Epistles; but there is still a marked difference between these two emphases.

Finally, the Epistles focus on the subject of love, calling readers to love and

> "And the Word became flesh and lived among us, and we have seen his glory, the glory as of a father's only son, full of grace and truth" (Jn 1:14).

> "We declare to you what was from the beginning, what we have heard, what we have seen with our eyes, what we have looked at and touched with our hands, concerning the word of life—²this life was revealed, and we have seen it and testify to it, and declare to you the eternal life that was with the Father and was revealed to us—" (1 Jn 1:1-2).

> "He is clothed in a robe dipped in blood, and his name is called The Word of God" (Rev. 19:13).

joy, and the same emphasis appears in the Fourth Gospel. In the case of Revelation, although its message is certainly one of joy for the victory of the Lamb, there is more emphasis on fear than on love. It is difficult to imagine the author of First John, who declares that "God is love," writing some of the harsh words of Revelation, or rejoicing at the fall of "Babylon the great," or proclaiming a victory that is wrought through catastrophic destruction and wholesale slaughter.

For all these reasons, most contemporary scholars think that these various parts of the Johannine corpus cannot have been written by the same person.

On the other hand, there are similarities among all three parts of the Johannine corpus that suggest a link among them. For instance, the declaration of the Fourth Gospel, that Jesus is the Incarnate Word of God (Jn 1:14), is echoed in the rest of the corpus (see 1 Jn 1:1-2; Rev. 19:13).

Secondly, while the imagery is not the same, there is in the entire corpus a constant contrast between good and evil, or between that which serves God and that which does not. In the Gospel it is the polarity between life and death, light and darkness, truth and falsehood, etc. As we shall see, there are similar polarities in the Epistles. And in Revelation there is the constant struggle between the dragon and the Lamb, and the stark contrast between those who conquer and those who yield to the powers of evil, or between those who worship the beast and those who worship God. Although commentators often refer to this as the "dualism" of the Johannine literature, we prefer to speak of "polarity," for in this entire corpus there is no sense that there is a principle of good and a principle of evil, or that some things are good and some are not. On the contrary, the God of all the Johannine literature in the New Testament is the creator of all things. There is no evil principle of creation. The Fourth Gospel begins with a declaration that "all things came into being through him, and without him not one thing came into being" (Jn 1:3). This is clear

"I looked, and there was a white horse! Its rider had a bow; a crown was given to him, and he came out conquering and to conquer. … And out came another horse, bright red; its rider was permitted to take peace from the earth, so that people would slaughter one another; and he was given a great sword. … I looked and there was a pale green horse! Its rider's name was Death, and Hades followed with him; they were given authority over a fourth of the earth, to kill with sword, famine, and pestilence, and by the wild animals of the earth" (Rev. 6:2, 4, 8).

throughout the Epistles of John, but it is equally true in Revelation. Indeed, in that book all evil is ultimately under God's control. This is the meaning of the passive voice that Revelation repeatedly employs to describe the power and authority of evil. For instance, we are told of the various riders of destruction that "a crown was given to him," that "its rider was permitted to take peace from the earth," and that "they were given authority" (Rev. 6:2, 4, 8). As we shall see, one of the main errors that First John rejects is the notion that material reality is evil, and that therefore the Savior cannot have come in the flesh.

Then, there are numerous images and phrases that appear both in the Gospel of John and in the Epistles—particularly First John. These include the view that salvation consists in "having life," the repeated use of terms such as "life," God being "light," Christian life as "walking in light," and many others.

Finally, there is the matter of the liturgical setting of the Gospel of John, Revelation, and First John. There is no doubt that in order to understand the Gospel of John one has to read it in the light of worship, and that most—if not all—of the book was written to be read out loud in the eucharistic gatherings of the early church. The same is true of Revelation. And, as we shall see, it is quite possible that First John, rather than an Epistle in the strict sense, is a treatise intended to be read to gathered congregations as they prepared to celebrate the Lord's Supper.

For all these reasons, many contemporary scholars, while agreeing that all these books were not written by a single author, argue that they are, however, the result of a common background and a common perspective on the Gospel. Some call this the "Johannine school," while others warn that the term "school" seems to imply a higher degree of connection than there actually was among the various writers of the Johannine corpus. Most likely, the commonalities binding these various writings together have to do with their emerging from the same region of the Mediterranean basin—a region in which Christianity had developed its own distinctive emphases.

Indeed, as one looks both at the New Testament and other early Christian literature, it would appear the area of what is today Turkey and Syria had developed its own distinctive theological perspectives.[1] Besides the Johannine writings, this perspective may be seen in the writings of the above-mentioned Papias of Hierapolis, as well as of Ignatius of Antioch, Polycarp of Smyrna (one of the cities whose churches Revelation addresses), Melito of Sardis (another such city), and Irenaeus of Lyon—who had actually grown up in Smyrna under the theological guidance of Polycarp. In all of these writings, as in much of the Johannine literature of the New Testament, one finds a number of common traits that indicate that Christians in that region did indeed look at Christianity in a particular way. Some of these characteristics are: First, a grand view of the cosmic significance of the Gospel. The Fourth Gospel is not content to begin with the ancestors of Jesus, as did Matthew and Luke, but goes back to the beginning of all things. Revelation presents the whole of history as a scroll closed with seven seals that only the victorious Lamb can open. Secondly, although God is the creator of all things, in the cosmic vision of this theological tradition there is a great struggle that goes even beyond the scope of history. The work of Jesus is to defeat the powers of evil, to be the light that casts out darkness, and the Gospel is a message of victory. Thirdly, there is an emphasis on the reality of the Incarnation. God did indeed become human, and every notion that the humanity of the Savior is not full humanity must be dispelled. Finally, while moral issues are crucial in this entire tradition, they are important because they are intimately related to the very nature of God and to God's victory over the powers of evil.

What can we say, then, about who wrote the three Epistles that we shall be studying? We can say with confidence that it was certainly not the author of Revelation, and most probably not the author of the Fourth Gospel. At the same time, we can say that the writer of the Epistles had much in common with those other writers. We can say that he (or she?) had deep roots in the Christianity of Asia Minor and the surrounding regions.

Can we say that his name was John? The text of the Epistles themselves does not say that such was the case. Actually, the writer prefers to refer to himself as "the elder." (The only book in the Johannine corpus whose author calls himself John is Revelation: "his servant John" [Rev. 1:1], "John to the seven churches" [Rev. 1:4].) But there is a very ancient tradition that speaks of a certain leader of the church in Ephesus whose name was indeed John, and which often attributes these letters to him. This tradition persisted through the ages, ever more embellished, to the point that it was said that if one visited John's tomb in Ephesus one could see the earth heave with his breathing! Even though much of this tradition is clearly legendary, the tradition itself is old enough that some suggest that there was indeed in the ancient church more than one leader by the name of John, and that the Epistles were written by one of them. Furthermore, as we shall see as we study First John, there are points at which some of the ancient traditions about John and his leadership may be of help in interpreting the Epistle itself.

In brief, it is impossible to tell with absolute certainty who the author of these three Epistles was. Since he calls himself "the elder," many commentators prefer to call him by that title. Here, for the sake of brevity and out of respect for the title that the Epistles now bear, we will call him John, although we are not implying by that name that he was also the author of either the Fourth Gospel or Revelation.

Do the three Epistles have a single author? Most probably. As one looks at early Christian references to them, sometimes the First Epistle is mentioned by itself; but the other two are never mentioned by themselves, as if they had circulated separately. The style and language of all three documents are sufficiently similar that they do seem to confirm that they are all the work of a single writer. Since the Second and Third Epistles are very brief, they probably derived their authority from their connection with the First, and eventually made their way into the canon of the New Testament on the basis of that connection. Indeed, from an early date there seems to have been a general consensus that First John was to be considered an inspired book, and worthy to be read in the worship of the church, while Second and Third John were often excluded. This was partly because in their brevity they did not seem to have much to say. When eventually they were included in the canon, this was because of their connection with First John. In a metaphor often used in politics, one could say that Second and Third John entered the canon of the New Testament on the coattails of First John.

When were these Epistles written? It is interesting to note that, while there is an undeniable similarity between First John and the Gospel of John, there is no literal quotation of either one in the other. The inevitable conclusion is that, even though the authors of these books belonged to the same theological tradition, each of them wrote independently. If, as is commonly assumed—but not universally held—the Epistle was written after the Gospel, it would seem that its author either did not know the Gospel or did not feel that its authority was such that it should be quoted as authoritative. And the same is true if one makes the opposite assumption, that the Epistle is earlier than the Gospel. No matter which was first, there must not have been sufficient time elapsing between their writing so that one author would quote the other. Then, there are allusions to First John in the Epistle of Polycarp, written in the early decades of the second century, and slightly later Papias of Hierapolis quotes it. For all these reasons, it seems logical to place the writing of the Epistle toward the end of the first century—which is also the most likely date for the Book of Revelation.

Having said all this, it is important to approach our study of the three Epistles of John—which will focus particularly on First John—as God's word to us today, in the early decades of the twenty-first century. We read these Epistles not simply because they provide information about the life and beliefs of the early church, but because they have something important to tell us; because we wish to be obedient to the will of God; because the Word of God to Christians in John's time is God's Word to Christians today.

We have quoted the negative comments of Isho'dad of Merv, who did not think that First John was sufficiently profound, or sufficiently elegant. His claims are solidly refuted, not just by other authors, but by the voice and the witness of thousands upon thousands of Christians through a span of twenty centuries who have heard God speaking to them in the Epistles of John. Among the many who contradict Isho'dad is John Wesley, who found the supposed simplicity of First John quite valuable, and who deplored the manner in which many preachers in his time confused complexity with profundity, and form with substance. On the 18th of July, 1765, Wesley wrote in his *Journal*:

> In the evening I began expounding the deepest part of the holy Scripture, namely, the first Epistle of St. John, by which, above all other, even inspired writings, I advise every young Preacher to form his style. Here are sublimity and simplicity together, the strongest sense and the plainest language! How

can one that would "speak as the oracles of God," use harder words than are found here?[2]

And what he told himself he also told others who would be preachers of the Word. In his prologue to a collection of his sermons, Wesley once again deplored the tendency of preachers to think that because their words were elegant they were good preachers, and to imitate the simplicity of First John:

> I think a preacher or a writer of Sermons has lost his way when he imitates any of the French orators, even the most famous. … Only let his language be plain, proper, and clear, and it is enough. God himself has told us how to speak, both as to the matter and the manner: "If any man speak," in the name of God, "let him speak as the oracles of God;" and if he would imitate any part of these above the rest, let it be the First Epistle of St. John. This is the style, the most excellent style, for every good preacher. And let him aim at no more ornament than he finds in that sentence, which is the sum of the whole gospel, "We love Him, because He first loved us."[3]

It was because God first loved him that John wrote these Epistles. It is because God first loved us that we now study them. It is because here we find God's love for all of us expressed in all its profound simplicity that we now invite you, dear reader, to enter with us into John's world, and with us to share his faith.

CHAPTER I
The Prologue: First John 1:1-4

Although it has traditionally been known as an Epistle, the document we are now studying lacks some of the characteristics of an ancient letter—and even of modern letters. If one looks, for instance, at the Epistles of Paul, or at the letter from the church in Jerusalem in Acts 15:23-30, we note that there is a parallel structure. These letters begin by identifying the sender—in the case of First Corinthians, "Paul, called to be an apostle ..." Then it names the addressees: "to the church of God that is in Corinth ..." This is followed by a salutation—"Grace to you and peace from God our Father and the Lord Jesus Christ"—and often a word of commendation—"I give thanks to my God always for you because ..." It is only after these preliminaries that the letter moves to the various subjects to be discussed. Finally, at the end of the letter there usually are personal notes and greetings—as in First Corinthians 16:15-21. First John has none of these characteristics. It plunges into its subject in its very first words. It never gives the names of the sender or of the intended readers.

There is no word of salutation or of commendation. And there are no personal greetings.

Given these characteristics, one would be inclined to think that what we have here is the text of a sermon or exhortation. But such an easy classification is thwarted by the clear declaration both at the beginning of the document (1 Jn 1:4) and at the end (1 Jn 5:13) that the author is writing.

It would thus seem that what we have here is something between a sermon and a letter. As a sermon, it speaks in general to its audience, although emphasizing points that are of particular concern to the preacher. As a letter, it has been written in order to circulate among the churches. It is an Epistle in the sense that it was to be sent and read to others. It is a universal or general Epistle in the sense that it seems to have been designed for wider circulation, and not for a single reading by a single recipient or group of recipients. But, unlike most Epistles, it tells us little or nothing about either the writer or the intended audience.

The text does not tell us who the "we" are who write, and who the "you" is who reads. At first it would seem that a clear distinction is being made between the "we" who have heard, seen, and touched, and the "you" who are to read the Epistle. Indeed, when it was commonly held that First John was written by the Apostle John, these opening words were seen as an assertion of the authority of the apostles—"we"—in communicating the gospel to others—"we declare to you." But as one reads the rest of the Epistle it becomes clear that the readers or hearers are included among those who have had the commandment of love from the beginning (2:7). This would seem to indicate that the author is including in his audience the "we" who have heard, seen, and touched. This view is supported further by the assertion in 1:4 that "*We* are writing these things so that *our* joy may be complete" (1:4)—to which we shall return shortly. Note also that in 1 John 1:4 these seem to be several people ("we are writing,") while in 1 John 5:13 there is a reference to a single author: "I write these things to you …"

As we look at the very beginning of the text, the NRSV has altered the order in which the various phrases appear in the Greek text of the Epistle, apparently seeking to make the sentence comply with the more common usage in English. The sentence thus begins with the subject, "we": "We declare to you what was from the beginning, what we have heard, what …"[4] In this respect, the NIV is closer to the original word order: "That which was from the beginning, which we have heard, which …—this we proclaim." While this does not change the meaning of the sentence, it does change the emphasis, which in the NRSV seems to shift from the events themselves to which John is referring to the "we" who write the letter. The entire passage is not primarily about the writer and the readers, but about "that which was from the beginning."

In the original order, the Epistle begins with "What was from the beginning," then connects this with three affirmations of physical constatation—"what we have heard … seen with our eyes … touched with our hands"—then explains the matter further—"this life was revealed … "—and only after all of this does the text say, "we declare to you."

To what "beginning" does this refer? Traditionally, the most common interpretation is that this is an apostle speaking of what he saw and heard during Jesus' lifetime on earth, particularly after the Resurrection, and now communicating it to others. But there are other possible interpretations. What Didymus the Blind reported in the fourth century has been true throughout most of the history of interpretation of this passage. According to Didymus, some believed that "the beginning" to which John refers is the beginning of the church, after the resurrection of Jesus; others connect the words with the Gospel of John, and take them as referring to the eternal Word of God, present with the Father from all ages; and a third group holds that John is affirming that believers have now seen with their own eyes what was prepared by God from the beginning.[5]

There is a clear parallelism between the prologue to First John and the prologue to the Gospel of John. Most scholars do not believe that the author of one of them had read the other, but rather that they both belong to the same strain in early Christian tradition, and therefore use similar phrases and images. In comparing the two prologues, one finds common phrases such as "what we have seen" or "what we have looked at," "the word," "life," and others. Of all these parallelisms, the most notable is the reference to "the beginning" at the very outset of the document. This would seem to indicate that both the author of the Gospel of John and the author of First John are referring to a commonly held emphasis in their particular strand of early Christianity, and that this is the emphasis on the grounding of the Gospel in the very nature of God, from the very beginning of all things. We know that at least by the middle of the second century, and probably much earlier, there were those who claimed that Christianity was a radically new thing, with no roots in the Hebrew faith. In fact, according to these people Christianity was so new that it had nothing to do with creation or with anything else that took place before the advent of Christ. Furthermore, the area where such doctrines seem to have been most common was the general area where the Johannine tradition flourished. The community that produced the most famous teacher of such doctrines, Marcion, was in the city of Sinope, on the southern coast of the Black Sea and therefore just north of the province of Asia, and this means that quite possibly there were already in Asia, decades before Marcion, those who proposed similar theories. Thus, both the Gospel of John and First John seem to be refuting any notion that the Gospel of Jesus Christ is a recent thing, something having nothing to do with what God was doing before the advent of Jesus. The Gospel of John does this from its very outset, declaring that it is the Word that was "in the beginning" that became incarnate in Jesus: "the Word became flesh and lived among us, and we have seen his glory" (Jn 1:14). First John expresses the same idea by asserting that "what was from the beginning" is also "what we have heard, what we have seen with our eyes, what we have looked at and touched with our hands."

Thus, by opening the document with the words "what was in the beginning," the author is showing a concern that is also clear in the Fourth Gospel. Of all four Gospels, only John grounds its story on the entire history of creation. Mark begins with the ministry of Jesus. Matthew places the story within the context of the history of Israel by beginning with a genealogy that goes all the way back to Abraham. Luke's genealogy goes farther, to Adam. But the Fourth Gospel opens with the radical declaration that "In the beginning was the Word." All of creation and all of history are part of a great cosmic drama whose climactic point is the life, death, resurrection, and coming reign of Jesus. Using very different imagery—a great book sealed with seven seals that only the Lamb can open—Revelation also affirms that all of history is a cosmic drama centering on the Lamb who was slain.

In brief, the phrase "what was in the beginning" does not mean simply at the beginning of the proclamation of the Gospel, but at the beginning of all things. While there is no indication that the writer of the Epistle had read the Fourth Gospel, by opening their works with a reference to the beginning both are bringing to mind the opening words of Genesis. First John is not speaking about something that happened yesterday, or a hundred years ago, or two thousand years ago. He is writing about something that has deep roots in the beginning of all things. "What was in the beginning" is none other than God. "In the beginning when God created the heavens and the earth" (Gn 1:1) implies that there is no other beginning than God. The same may be seen in the prologue to the Gospel of John: "In the beginning was the Word, and the Word was with God" (Jn 1:1). Now First John begins by making it clear that this is not about something that has happened lately, nor is it strictly speaking about the teachings of the church or about Christian behavior. Such things have a place in the proclamation of the church; but the heart of that proclamation has to be what was in the beginning—God.

Having understood this, and seen its connection with the eternal reality of God that is in the very beginning, John jars us with what would seem to be the utterly preposterous statement that he and those who share his faith have heard, seen, and even touched that which—or rather, the One who—was in the beginning! As we shall see, John seems to have been concerned that there were those who called themselves Christians, but sought to soften the edges of such a statement. Yet, this is also what the Fourth Gospel says when, after speaking of the greatness of the Word, and of the identity of the Word with God, it too makes the shocking statement that "the Word became flesh."

Augustine, the famous saint and theologian of the late fourth and early fifth centuries who was well versed in the philosophies of his times, said that just about everything that the Fourth Gospel says about the Word he had been able to find in the writings of the philosophers, but that the one thing he did not find there was the statement in verse 14: "the Word became flesh."[6] In that report, Augustine was simply stating what is obvious to any reader of the Fourth Gospel or of First John: that the One who was in the beginning was made flesh is at the very heart of the Christian message. As First John would put it, "this we proclaim concerning the Word of life" (1 Jn 1:1, NIV).

It is not enough to affirm the fact of the Incarnation. That God entered into human life is not simply a doctrine. The Gospel adds that the Incarnate Word "dwelt among us." The Epistle adds that those who were with Jesus touched him with their hands. In other words, the importance of the fact that God took on human form was that God wished to be with us, with us in a radical way, to share our human life, to be one of us. In Jesus, God did not stand apart from human beings, but could actually be touched. There is more than doctrine here. There is the basis for all of the words about the love God has for us that will follow in this letter. It is God's love for us, the desire for nearness to us, that led to the Incarnation. And this is the prelude to the possibility of our nearness to God. In Revelation 21:3, in the picture of the heavenly Jerusalem we read that "the home of God is among mortals. He will dwell with them as their God." Thus, all the Johannine corpus in the New Testament stresses the Incarnation as God's dwelling among us—a dwelling that will find its fulfilment in the final day.

The reference to "the Word of life" has two layers of meaning. To us, the most obvious meaning is the message that Christians proclaim, which is a message that brings life to its hearers. This is certainly true, and the first readers of First John would understand it. But such readers, acquainted as they must have been with the emphases of the Johannine tradition, would understand more. In the Gospel of John, the Word is that through which all things were made. The Word harkens back to the beginning of creation and even before. The Word is God's creative power; it is God acting and creating. Since in Greek "Word" is *logos*, and this was a term commonly used in Hellenistic philosophy, it has often been thought that this is something the Fourth Gospel draws from Hellenistic rather than Jewish traditions. But scholars have modified such views, pointing to the Jewish roots of what the Fourth Gospel says. In Genesis, God creates through the Word: "God said, 'Let there be ... and there was ... '"! Since the Word is God's creative power, what God speaks leaps into existence. The Word is the source of all things. But even more, the Word is the source of life: "in him was life" (Jn 1:4). In conclusion, when First John speaks of "the Word of life," this does not mean only the message that brings life to sinners, but also the very power behind all things and all life. Once again, "what we have heard, what we have seen with our eyes, what we have looked at and touched with our hands" has to do with what was from the beginning, with the power behind all creation and all life.

Verse 2 links "what was from the beginning," and what "we have seen," with the appropriate response: we "testify to it, and declare to you the eternal life." To testify is to render witness, to declare what one has seen or heard, and is therefore a most appropriate word here. This word also provides a clue as to the nature of John's message. One does not testify to self-evident, nor to purely abstract, truths. If some people declare that two times two is four, they are not testifying; they are simply stating a permanent truth, and one that can be known to anyone who simply looks at reality. There certainly is an element of empirical corroboration in such a statement, for we can take two stones and two other stones and find that we now have four. But still we do not say that someone who declares that two times two is four is a witness. Such a person might be a teacher, but not a witness. Witnessing requires a connection with historical data. In a court of law, witnesses are those who declare what they have seen or heard. The same is true in First John. Here, testifying or witnessing is much more than simply asserting what anyone in any circumstance could know. It is proclaiming events that one could see, hear, and touch (v. 1). Therefore, John's truth is not a proposition nor a series of propositions. Nor is it a doctrine or a series of doctrines. It may well require certain propositions and doctrines; but it is something that has been seen, heard, and even touched. To this we shall return later (see commentary on 4:8).

One should also note that here "eternal life" does not mean only the promise believers have of life everlasting. In verse 2 we read that the message that is being proclaimed is much more than that. It is no less than "the eternal life that was with the Father and was revealed to us." Beyond life everlasting for individuals, "eternal life" is the very nature of God. It is God who lives eternally, and it is out of this eternal life and its love that everlasting life flows into us as creatures of the God who is life.

When we come to this point in the reading of the text, we begin to realize that in these four short verses there are several words that appear repeatedly. The words "we have seen"—a single word in Greek—appear three times. "Life" appears three times; and "was revealed" twice—as does also "fellowship." The phrase "and declare to you" is used in verse 2 and almost immediately again in verse 3. Were we to send to a publisher a manuscript with such repetitions of words in the same paragraph, the copy editor would have a ball with it! Normally, such repetition of words is not considered good style. But First John appears to be doing this on purpose. The repetition of exactly the same words—or the same verb in the same tense—shows the concatenation of ideas. C. Clifton Black has expressed this quite well in *The New Interpreter's Bible* by calling these "verbal batons [that] are transferred from one clause ... to the next."[7] The preface thus has the structure of a relay race, in which one sentence or clause picks up some of the batons of the previous ones, and in so doing carries the idea forward. The same is true of much of the Epistle.

As we approach the end of the prologue, we are told the reasons why the entire document is being written. The first is "that you may have fellowship with us." The second is "that our joy may be complete."

The word usually translated as "fellowship"—*koinonia*—means much more than that. To us, "fellowship" means a sense of community, of enjoying one another's presence. We thus have "fellowship halls" in our churches, and these are places where we gather to have activities that promote our unity, to share fun and meals, and in general for everything except worship, which takes place in the sanctuary. But in ancient times the word *koinonia* meant much more than that. A *koinonia* was more like our modern-day corporations. Partners in a business were termed *koinonoi*—members of a *koinonia*. Therefore, when John speaks of his readers having "fellowship with us" he does not mean only that they may feel as one. He means also that they may be members of a partnership—perhaps even a corporation. They have a common property, a common inheritance, a common promise. And, most surprisingly, it is not only among themselves that Christians have this partnership, but also "with the Father and with his Son Jesus Christ." These are astounding words! John is inviting his readers to become partners in a corporation headed no less than by God! Presumably, the assets of this corporation include all that belongs to God! If this seems exaggerated, it is no more than what Paul also says: "For all things are yours, whether Paul or Apollos or Cephas or the world or life or death or the present or the future—all belong to you, and you belong to Christ, and Christ belongs to God" (1 Cor. 3:21-23).

In order to understand the full impact of such words, we must remember that all indications are that most of the members of both the Johannine and the Pauline communities were poor people. Many were slaves. Others had to struggle for survival. Those who had occupations ruled by guilds—carpenters, masons, smiths, and many others—might well be expelled from such guilds when they refused to worship the gods of the guild. The people gathered in church to hear the reading of First John most likely had risen before dawn to go to the Christian gathering, for they would have to go to work with the rising of the sun. And these people are now being told that they are partners with God in the all-embracing corporation of all creation and all eternity!

John's purpose in writing the letter is that his readers may be part of this *koinonià*; that they may share in what John has, and this is nothing less than eternal life—not just everlasting life, but the very God who *is* life eternal.

But, while in the common usage the Greek word *koinonia* meant corporation or partnership, for Christians it also meant communion—the celebration of the Lord's Supper that was the high point of Christian worship. Communion was named *koinonia* because through it Christians became partners in the body of Christ, and also because the early communion services were occasions of sharing in which all brought what they could, and in that particular moment, as in a foretaste of the Reign of God, none would be hungry.

When we reflect on it, it is interesting to note that the one thing that we never do in our fellowship—*koinonia*—halls is precisely that which the early church considered the highest expression and source of their *koinonia*. Why is this? Could it be that we are more comfortable with a "fellowship" that is based on our liking one another, on our belonging to the same social class, the same culture, and so on, rather than in our belonging to the One to whom all things belong, and who belongs to us? At this point, one is reminded of the words of an ancient Christian writer—probably John's contemporary—who said: "If we share in things eternal, are we not to share in things temporal?"[8]

Then, there is a second purpose to John's writing: "so that our joy may be complete." It is interesting to note that there are several ancient manuscripts that say "your joy" rather than "our joy." A careful comparison of various groups or families of manuscripts leads to the conclusion that the original text said "*our* joy," but also that at a relatively early date some copyists wrote "your joy" instead of "our joy," and thus their text says "we write to you so that *your* joy may be complete." In Greek, as in English, the difference between "your" and "our" is a single letter, and therefore it is easy to read one for the other—particularly when the sense of the text seems to lead in that direction. Apparently, some copyists felt that it made more sense for John to write so that the joy of his readers could be complete, than to write in order to complete his own joy. Even if, as is most likely, the original text said our joy, one could ask whether the "we" whose joy will be complete is the "we" who write the Epistle, or it is a wider "we," including both those who write and those who read.

When we stop to consider the matter, the two are not mutually exclusive. John writes so that both he and his readers may rejoice. These two are two sides of the same coin. Those who hear rejoice in their hearing, and those who proclaim rejoice in their proclamation. These two sides of the coin are expressed in two very similar hymns that were quite popular a few decades ago. The first expresses the need to hear the story over and over again, and the joy in such hearing: "Tell me the old, old story of unseen things above, of Jesus and his glory, of Jesus and his love." The other expresses the joy in telling the story: "I love to tell the story of unseen things above, of Jesus and his glory, of Jesus and his love." Significantly, these two hymns were sung by congregations with the same joy, and often without even noticing the two different emphases, one on hearing, and the other on telling. Like-wise, when John writes, he expects that his message will cause joy in those who read, and also that he too will rejoice in the very telling of it. And, in the very telling, the "we" has broadened so as to include both those who proclaim and those who hear—or read.

John opens the Epistle with the recital of the essential elements of the Gospel that both his church and his readers affirm. Such reaffirmation may be there because there is a danger that the readers may forget it. He then concludes that the joy of his own church is complete when both churches are joined in fellowship. This would be because they not only adhere to the same Gospel but they are one church in Christ. If in spite of those who deny the Incarnation John's readers remain faithful to the true Gospel, the joy of all true believers will be complete.

CHAPTER 2
Light and Darkness; Sin and Confession:
First John 1:5–2:2

The "baton" passed from the previous passage to this one, linking the two together, appears in verse 5: "the message we have heard from him and proclaim to you." The connection between this and the preceding is double. First, there is the verb "we have heard," which appeared earlier in verses 1 and 3. Second, the verb "we proclaim" (*anangellomen*) shares the same root with the verb in the earlier section that the NRSV translates as "we declare" (*apangellomen*); and that root is in the word *angellia*, translated here as "message." This is the same root as in *euangellion*, gospel, meaning good news.

In the prologue, John has told his readers that he has something to proclaim to them as a witness, that this was from the beginning and has now been heard, seen, and touched. There, we were told little about this "something" that was in the beginning, and that has been seen and heard.

This will clearly be the subject of the entire writing. But in the prologue it is characterized simply as "that which"—that which was from the beginning—or as "what"—what we have heard, what we have seen, what we have looked at, what we have touched. Now, in verse 5, that something is called a "message"—an *angellia*.

The declaration that what the Epistle is about is a "message" fits with the earlier description of those who have seen and heard as witnesses. A message usually has to do with events, either past, present, or future. When it has to do with the past, a message is most often news about something that has happened—as, for instance, "the enemy has landed." When it has to do with the present, it often changes our perspective on things—for instance, "William is spying for the enemy." When it has to do with the future, it often is a commandment—for instance, "have William arrested." Thus, messages usually have to do with events, with changed perspectives, or with commandments or instruction. Again, "two times two is four" is true; but it hardly is a message.

It is important to understand this, for it helps us see what John means by declaring that the content of the message is "God is light and in him there is no darkness at all." Were we to read such these words by themselves, they would seem to be no more than a declaration as to the eternal nature of God. They certainly are that. Over the centuries many philosophers and theologians have asserted that the best way to speak about the Supreme Being is by analogies which apply to God what we deem to be positive features—beauty, goodness, strength—and asserting that these apply to the divine in a superlative way. Reading this passage as such an assertion, many have written profound and inspiring words about how God is. But John is going beyond that. John is not speaking about God in static terms, trying to define or describe the divine. John is speaking about how God relates to creation, and about how the creation—particularly the human creature—is to respond to this God who is light.

The declaration that God is light and in him there is no darkness therefore leads directly to a statement as to how humans are to act. Human behavior is described metaphorically in terms of walking—just as today we are told that it is not enough to "talk the talk," and that we have to "walk the walk." And here we come to one of those polarities or radical alternatives that characterize the entire Johannine corpus. There are two alternatives, and no other: one must either walk in light or walk in darkness. Just as earlier verses in First John showed a series of parallelisms with the prologue to the Gospel of John, so does this image of the contrast between light and darkness. Thus we read in John 1:5 that "The light shines in the darkness, and the darkness did not overcome it."

This image of life as walking is probably quite old, and must have been common in John's time. In two ancient and apparently not interdependent Christian writings, the *Didache* and the *Epistle of Barnabas* (the first probably written at about the same time as First John, and the latter a few decades later) we are told that there are two paths: the path of life and the path of death. Here John tells us that there are two ways of walking: in light and in darkness. Significantly, however, while both the *Didache* and the *Epistle of Barnabas* speak primarily of the place to which the two alternative paths lead—life and death—John speaks of the reason why believers are to choose a particular way of walking—in light. There is no reference here to rewards or punishment, or to living or dying depending on which way one walks. This is not denied; but such consequences are not the reason for choosing to walk in light. The ultimate reason for walking in light is that God is light. Walking in darkness must be avoided simply because there is no darkness in God—not because it leads to death or to punishment, as in the *Didache* and the *Epistle of Barnabas*, or even in Matthew 7:13-14.

Now follow a series of six sentences beginning with "if." These can be paired into three sets of which the first "if" presents an alternative to be rejected, and the second "if" offers the positive alternative. The first element of each of these pairs—the negative "if"—has to do with what we claim about ourselves: "if we say that we ... " (1:6, 8, 10), and all have to do with claiming that we are what we are not. The second part of each set—the second, fourth, and sixth "ifs"—presents the positive alternative to each of the "ifs" preceding it: "if we walk in the light" (1:7), "if we confess" (1:9), and "we have an advocate" (2:1). While each pair of "ifs" has its own emphasis, they are quite repetitive, and can best be understood as musical composition in which the same theme appears repeatedly, but each time more sharply defined and in crescendo.

The first negative "if" connects with the prologue by returning to the theme of fellowship (*koinonia*). In this new section, however, the order is reversed. In 1:3 John moved from "fellowship with us" to fellowship with God. Now he begins with fellowship with God, and "fellowship with one another" will be left for the second set of "ifs." In this first set, what one may say is that one has fellowship with God: "If we say, we have fellowship with God … " There is nothing wrong with that! This should be the goal of every believer. The problem is in not being consequent with such a claim. What is wrong is to claim that one has fellowship with God, and then to walk "in darkness."

John does not tell us exactly what he means by such "walking in darkness." The image appears repeatedly in ancient literature, and its meaning is twofold. First, walking in darkness is what people do when they do not wish to have their actions known. It often refers to actions such as murder, thieving, and adultery, which become easier under cover of darkness. In this usage, the image has a moral emphasis: walking in darkness is doing what one should not do. But then walking in darkness also means to be lost and in danger. Most of us have seldom really walked in darkness. Our streets have at least minimal illumination. In our homes we have night lights. Therefore, we seldom stumble because it is dark. But things were very different in ancient times. Only a few small areas were illumined by torches. When the night was dark, without stars or moonlight, one practically had to grope along the way. There was always danger of stepping into a hole or losing one's way. And there was also the danger of ambush and violence. If one carried a light, that did not help much. While it might keep you from stumbling or losing your way, it also made it easier for robbers and other evildoers to see you, and more difficult for you to see them. This is why those who could afford it had others—usually slaves—carrying torches ahead of them. Many of those reading First John would have firsthand experience of the terrors of walking in darkness. Since most of them were not masters of their own lives, they would most likely come to the congregational meeting long before sunrise, in the small hours of the morning, precisely the time when the darkness is deepest and danger most threatening. They would know what John was talking about when he spoke of walking in darkness!

But the very fact that they were in church, listening to the reading of this Epistle, would mean that at least they claimed to have fellowship with God. This would be particularly true at that time, when there was no prestige nor social advantage in church participation. Since "fellowship" (*koinonia*) means partnership, sharing, having things in common, to have fellowship with God meant more than praying or being a friend of God. It meant also sharing in the nature and the truth of God. If, as John has just said, "God is light," one cannot have fellowship with God without sharing in the divine light. In this context, walking in light is not just a matter of something one should or ought to do. It is being what one claims to be: someone who shares in the divine light.

All of this means that John is not just calling on his readers to do what is right or to avoid doing evil. He is telling them to be what they say they are: partners in *koinonia* with God. Those who are not really such, yet claim to be, are liars who "do not do what is true." This leads us to another of those typically Johannine polarities, this time the polarity between truth and falsehood.

Note, however, that this lying does not consist merely in telling an untruth. John says "we lie and we do not do what is true." Just as the message that John proclaims is not a series of propositions, so is the evil that he is decrying not merely saying something that is not true. In a narrow sense, lying is telling an untruth, and those who claim to be in fellowship with God but walk in darkness are clearly lying. But they also "do not do what is true." Here truth is not just something one says, nor even something one believes; truth is something one is and one does. Truth is a state and an action rather than a proposition. Truth is authenticity.

The counterpart of walking in darkness—the second half of this first pair of "ifs"—is walking "in the light, as he himself is in the light." This immediately leads us back to the very nature of God as it was described in 1:5: "God is light." But this positive "if" is not exactly parallel to its negative counterpart. We would expect John to say that if we walk in light we have fellowship with God. But John surprises us in two ways. First of all, instead of speaking about fellowship with God, he now speaks of "fellowship with one another." Later, in the second chapter, John will argue that love of God is manifested in loving others. Here he announces that theme by moving from "fellowship with God" in the first "if" to "fellowship with one another" in the second "if." In so doing, he gives us a hint of how he will later clarify what he means by "walking in the light." Having fellowship with God cannot be separated from having fellowship with one another. As John Wesley would put it, there is "no holiness but social holiness."[9] Walking in the light is to have *koinonia* with one another—and let us not forget what was said above to the effect that *koinonia* implies partnership, sharing, commonality. This is why in the third century a distinguished leader of the church, Cyprian of Carthage, declared that one cannot have God as Father without having the church as mother.[10] By this he was not trying to promote the church as an organization, nor to call believers to obedience to the church, but simply stating what John says here, that fellowship with God and fellowship with one another cannot be separated.

The other way in which John surprises us in this second "if" is by speaking of "sin." He has not even used the word up to this point. Now, with no further introduction of the matter, John declares that if we live in light not only do we have fellowship with one another, but also "the blood of Jesus his [God's] Son cleanses us from all sin." There is no further explanation here as to how the blood of Jesus purifies, but the connotations of the phrase may lead us in two different but parallel directions: on the one hand, it may refer to the long-standing tradition in the Law of Israel of purification by means of ritual sacrifice; on the other, "blood" is the equivalent of life, and therefore it is possible to read these words as referring to the life of Jesus, and not only to his death—in which case John is returning to his earlier theme of the eternal life that has been revealed.

In any case, the theme of sin, introduced for the first time at the end of the first pair of "ifs," serves as a link to introduce the second pair, which begins with "if we say that we have no sin." As one compares this second set of "ifs" with the first set, one notes that, while appearing to repeat what the first set said, it actually moves the argument further. On the negative side, the lie is not only to others, in presenting ourselves falsely; it is also in that "we deceive ourselves" (1:8). And not only do we not "do" the truth (1:6); but rather, "the truth is not in us" (1:8). On the positive side, it is not now a matter of what we do or how we walk, but rather of confessing: "if we confess our sins … " (1:9). In the first pair of "ifs," we were called to do something, to walk in a certain way. In this second half, we are not told to do anything but confess. And, at the end of this second set of "ifs," the theme of cleansing from sin appears once again, thus serving as one of those "batons" that various sections of the Epistle seem to hand to the following section so as to provide continuity in the discourse.

This progression continues in the third set of "ifs." At this point the Epistle becomes more personal, repeatedly addressing its intended readers with terms of endearment: "little children" (2:1; 3:18; 5:21), "beloved" (2:7; 4:1, 7), and "children" (2:18). On the negative side of this third set of "ifs," John declares that if we say that we have no sin we not only deceive others and ourselves, but we even make God a liar, and "his word"—again, a repetition of a theme that appeared in the prologue—is not in us. On the positive side, in this third set it is no longer a matter of what we do, as in the first set, or of what we say, as in the second, but simply of what God does. John seems to break the rhythm of "ifs" with the comment in 2:1, that he is writing so that his readers—"my little children—will not sin. But this is only the introduction to the positive side of the third set. Before moving into his final "if," which is an announcement of the grace and love of God, John makes sure that this is not taken as an invitation to sin. This is similar to Paul's concern when he too is discussing the love of God, who graciously forgives sin: "What then are we to say? Should we continue in sin in order that grace may abound? By no means!" (Rom. 6:1-2). So, having made certain that his readers will not be misguided into thinking that John is saying that sin is not grievous, John comes to his final "if." He has been exhorting his readers to act properly by walking in light, to speak properly by confessing their sins, and now he concludes the entire section with a final and radical affirmation of God's grace and love: "if anyone does sin, we have an advocate … " (2:1). The term translated here as "advocate" is "paraclete," the same that Jesus gives both himself and the Spirit in the Gospel of John: "I will ask the Father, and he will give you another Advocate, to be with you forever" (Jn 14:16)—which once again points to the common theological traditions behind the Fourth Gospel and the First Epistle of John.

In conclusion, while the entire passage is a call not to sin, it is also and even more a proclamation of the grace of God for us sinners. While it bemoans the enormity of sin, it calls us to trust in a grace that is even greater. As John Calvin put it …

> In short, John means that we are not only called away from sin by the gospel, because God invites us to himself, and offers to us the Spirit of regeneration, but that a provision is made for miserable sinners, that they may have God always propitious to them, and that the sins by which they are entangled, do not prevent them from becoming just, because they have a Mediator to reconcile them to God. The intercession of Christ is a continual application of his death for our salvation. That God then does not impute to us our sins, this comes to us, because he has regard to Christ as intercessor.[11]

CHAPTER 3
Love and Obedience: First John 2:3-17

The next section underscores what has already been said about authenticity, but now it introduces three new themes: knowledge (2:3), commandments (2:3), and love (2:5). The usage of the verb "to know" in this Epistle deserves particular attention. In Spanish—as in Latin and in many other Romance languages—there are two different verbs that are translated into English as "to know." One—*conocer*—means to know in the sense of being acquainted with something or someone, while the other—*saber*—means to know as one knows a fact or a proposition. In English we make that distinction with the word "that." One "knows" a person; one "knows that" a person is good, or that two times two makes four. In verse 3, John is referring to knowing in the first of these two senses: "we know him."

This distinction is important, because quite possibly John is rejecting the view of some who held that salvation is by a secret knowledge or *gnosis*—for which reason they came to be known as "Gnostics." Although we do not know to what stage Gnosticism had developed in John's time, we do know that a few decades later most Christian teachers saw it as a serious threat to Christianity. Therefore, it is possible that in this section John is envisioning an earlier form of what would soon develop into Christian Gnosticism. The "knowledge" that the Gnostics claimed was propositional. It was not a matter of knowing God, but rather of knowing certain things about oneself—and in some cases of knowing the secret passwords that would allow the soul to pass through the celestial spheres and into the highest heaven. But John claims that knowing God is something altogether different. It is not a matter of knowing something about God, or about the heavenly spheres; it is a matter of knowing God.

There is a vast difference between these two, even though they are inter-related. When a child knows its mother, it obviously knows something about her. It knows, for instance, *that* her name is Susan, *that* she is a lawyer, *that* she is tall. All these points, and many others, may be true; but all of this pales in comparison with simply knowing her. It is much more important for a child to know its mother than to know something about her. And the place where knowing her and knowing about her meet is in knowing *that* she loves the child. But there is more. When a child truly knows its mother, it also knows its mother's values, the way she would like and expect the child to be and to behave. Thus, knowing the mother, the child also knows *that* there are certain things it must do and certain others it must not do.

All of this helps us understand John's words in verse 3: "we may be sure that we know him, if we obey his commandments." As will be made clear in the rest of the Epistle, the commandments to which John refers are not some collection of capricious demands established by God; it is rather the commandment to be like God—and more specifically, to love as God loves. The Gnostics may claim all sorts of knowledge about God; but if they do not obey God—if they do not love as God loves—, they do not know God. The most orthodox theologian may know all the right doctrines about God; but knowing God goes beyond doctrine, for it is a matter of obedience—and specifically, of obedience made manifest in love.

As in the previous section, John makes this point by a series of hypothetical statements. In Greek, however, there are different ways of expressing such hypothetical statements, and the form employed here implies a higher degree of probability than the "if" statements in the previous section. This is why the NRSV translates the hypothetical subject of these three sentences as "whoever." Thus, verses 4-6 present three such hypothetical statements. Verse 4 presents the negative option; verse 5 presents its positive counterpart; and verse 6 invites readers to opt for obedience. All of these hypothetical statements are connected with the earlier "ifs" by the themes of truth and falsehood (v. 4), and of the manner in which one walks as a sign of truth and faithfulness (v. 5). Taken together, their main thrust is the connection between faith and obedience. John does not say whether those whom he calls "liars" are such because they lack faith or because they lack obedience. Is it that one does not really believe, and therefore one does not obey? Or is it rather that one does not wish to obey, and therefore one refuses to believe? Dietrich Bonhoeffer wrote some profound observations on the relationship between these two:

> This situation may be described by two propositions, both of which are equally true. Only one who believes is obedient, and only he who is obedient believes. …

> For faith is only real when there is obedience, never without it, and faith only becomes faith in the act of obedience. …

> If we are to believe, we must obey a concrete command. Without this preliminary step of obedience, our faith will be only pious humbug.[12]

It is here, in verse 5, that the word "love" appears for the first time in First John. It will be used fifty-one other times—and then again ten more times in Second and Third John. Surprisingly, however, it appears in the ambiguous phrase that the NRSV correctly translates as "the love of God."

This may mean two different things. On the one hand, it may mean the love God has for us—as when we say that "the love of God is all-encompassing." On the other, it may mean our love for God—as when we say that someone did something extraordinary "for the love of God." This may seem puzzling, for we would like John to be absolutely clear in every detail, and ambiguities make it difficult for us to pin him down. But the ambiguity may be quite purposeful, for the main thrust of the entire letter is that love is reciprocal; that we love God because God first loved us; that God's love for us spills over into God's love for all of creation; and that our love of God must be manifested in love for all those whom God loves. The ambiguity of the phrase itself thus points to the impossibility to contain love within the limits of our definitions or classifications.

Then, the context in which the phrase "the love of God" appears enriches it even further: "in this person the love of God has reached perfection." Again, this may mean that such a person loves God perfectly. And it may also mean that God's love for such a person has reached its goal, that one now is what God wills one to be. There has been much discussion as to what Wesley meant by "being perfected in love." Here, First John seems to imply that this is perfection both in the sense of perfectly loving God and in the sense of being the result of God's perfect love. And, no matter whether it is one or the other, there is no doubt that there is here a call to love God with all of one's self—to seek to be perfected in love.

There are overtones here of the great affirmation of Judaism: "Hear, O Israel: The Lord is our God, the Lord alone. You shall love the Lord your God with all your heart, and with all your soul, and with all your might" (Deut. 6:4-5).

Finally, before moving on to verse 7, it is important to note that here we have the first instance of a phrase or image that will appear repeatedly in this and some other Johannine literature: Christian life as "abiding" in God or being "in him"—sometimes meaning in God, and sometimes in Jesus, as in verse 6. Just as knowing God is more than merely knowing *that* God exists, being *in* God—or in Christ—is more than believing certain things about God. It is making God the very foundation and the entire context of the manner in which one lives. It does not mean, as some mystical traditions claim, that we disappear in God. It means rather that by being in God we truly appear, we truly become what we are (see a similar idea in Col. 3:3-4).

When we come to verses 7 and 8, John's words puzzle us once again. He says first, "I am writing you no new commandment, but an old commandment," and then, in the very next verse, he seems to contradict himself: "Yet I am writing you a new commandment." The apparent contradiction is so blatant that it must have been purposeful. It cannot be simply that John forgot what he has just said. It is rather that this commandment is such that it is old, and at the same time it is new. As the rest of the Epistle will make abundantly clear, this commandment that is both old and new is the commandment of love. This is the "commandment that you have had from the beginning" (v. 7). Here, as in 1:1, "the beginning" is both the beginning of their faith, when they were first called, and the beginning of all things— "the beginning" to which Genesis 1:1 and John 1:1 refer, and with which First John opens. Love is nothing new. It is as old as the hills—and even older. Later, John will declare that "God is love." Love is the force behind all of creation. And yet, the commandment of love is always renewed. It is never something we have already heard, and heard sufficiently. There is no déjà vu here. Love is always fresh, for the love that called all things out of nothing still calls us to be that which God intends us to be. Furthermore, the advent of Christ makes this commandment ever more urgent, and in that sense new, because "the darkness is passing away and the true light is already shining." These last words remind us both of the earlier imagery of light and darkness, and of what the Gospel of John declares, that "the light shines in the darkness, and the darkness did not overcome it" (Jn 1:5).

The reintroduction of the theme of light and darkness in verse 8 adds an important dimension to previous references to that theme. Here there is a temporal urgency: "the true light is already shining." Although God as light is eternal, something has happened that has brought new light into the world. This "something" is the advent of Jesus and the birth of the church. As the Fourth Gospel declares, Jesus is the true light that has come into the world, and therefore those who follow him must live under that true and new light. But, once again, this light is not a matter of mere "enlightenment"—of knowing something that we did not know. It is a matter of walking in the light. And this walking takes the concrete shape of love. Significantly, John's new and old commandment is not a negative list of prohibitions, nor even a positive list of directions as to things to do. It is simply the principle of love. Those who follow this principle walk in light; those who do not, walk in darkness, as if they were blind (2:11).

In verses 12-14 we have John's clear statement of the diversity of people to whom he is writing. He does this by means of three sets of addresses in terms of their ages: little children, fathers (which may mean parents), and young people. Each of these groups is addressed twice. Interestingly, in the case of "fathers" what is said in verse 13 is simply repeated in verse 14. It was customary in ancient societies to classify people according to their ages, giving each age particular rights and duties. What John says here to each of these groups can be related to the specific experiences of each age: the children are forgiven and they know the Father; the fathers, who are the beginning of a family, "know him who is from the beginning"; and the young ones are addressed in terms of strength and victory. But in spite of those different emphases, the main thrust of this repeated triple address is to include all in the message of the letter. In other places in the New Testament (for instance, Eph. 5:22–6:9) people are addressed separately, each group with a particular word to it—husbands and wives, fathers and children, slaves and masters. Here the emphasis is in the opposite direction. Each age may emphasize and experience different conditions and concerns; but the Epistle is equally addressed to all.

In the context of the preceding emphasis on love, the implication is clear. There may be different age groups in the community of faith—and, by implication, other groups on the basis of gender, culture, etc. But they are all part of the same community, and the commandment of love applies to all of them—particularly across group lines. The children are told to love the adults and the young ones; the fathers, to love the children and the young ones; and the young ones, to love the fathers and the children.

After these tripartite addresses, John turns to the negative side of love. Later he will return to love, and to its beauty and power. But first he has to make clear that not all love is good: "Do not love the world or the things in the world" (2:15). Such love he contrasts with "the love of the Father," and John declares that the two are radically incompatible: "The love of the Father is not in those who love the world."

When we read these words, we tend to think that "the world" is the material things around us, and that John is saying that we should not love such things, but only the spiritual or immaterial. This is due to a common assumption that religion has to do with things unseen, and that therefore things that are seen have nothing to do with it, and may even oppose it. But this is not what John is saying. He has already declared that there is an indissoluble connection between God of love and love of others. Later, in 3:17, he will make it clear that this has to do with making use of the world's goods to respond to the needs of a brother or sister. These are physical as well as spiritual needs. Thus, things are not necessarily evil, for they can be used as instruments of love, to meet human need. Nor is the body or the flesh necessarily evil. Later on, John will insist on the truth that "Jesus has come in the flesh" (4:2). In the Fourth Gospel, we read that God loved the world (Jn 3:16; a phrase that finds echoes in 1 Jn 2:2; 4:9, 14). And throughout Scripture we are told that all things, physical and not, are the creation of God. Therefore, things in themselves are not evil, and the physical world is not evil.

John's meaning becomes clearer when we remember that he has been promoting love of others: "Whoever loves a brother or sister lives in the light." Thus, the admonition in 2:15, not to love the world or the things of

"For God so loved the world that he gave his only Son, so that everyone who believes in him may not perish but may have eternal life " (Jn 3:16).

the world, means that such must not be the object of love, but should rather be placed at the service of love for others. Love of things over people is a condition in which desire for self-gratification overcomes love of neighbor. This John expresses by referring to three forms of desire: "the desire of the flesh, the desire of the eyes, the pride in riches." Most commentators do not think that John is here listing three different types, objects, or sources of desire, but rather making it clear that he is referring to the general nature of the "world" whose love he opposes. Note that "all that is in the world" is not explained with a list of material things—animals, plants, bodies, etc.—but with a description of "desire." The word translated here as "desire" (*epithymia*) usually has a negative connotation. It is not merely a wish or a yearning; it is a controlling drive, almost like a torrent that will allow nothing to stand in its way. In Hellenistic ethical writings, it is often opposed to rational, controlled action. The "flesh" does not mean the body, but rather the desire of the creature not to be such, the rebellion of the creature against its creator, the boundless desire not only for self-gratification, but also for autonomy. Thus, the love for the world that John here contrasts with the love of the Father is not just love of material things, but rather a rebellious attitude that places itself above and beyond the reaches of obedience and dependence from God, and that even seeks to use and rule all of creation as if one were the creator, and not part of creation itself.

In short, "love of the world" is the attitude of those who live according to the negative options presented earlier in the series of "ifs" (1:6–2:1) and in the ensuing series beginning with "whoever" (2:4-6). But in contrast to those other passages, the emphasis here lies on the negative, on the alternative to the love of God, on that which is to be avoided. This serves as an introduction to the section that follows, where John will make it clear that there are those who oppose his teachings, and that he feels these people are a threat to the community of love.

The entire section ends with an affirmation that reminds us of the Book of Revelation: "the world and its desire are passing away, but those who do the will of God live forever." If "the darkness is passing away and the true light is already shining" (2:8), and if "the world and its desire are passing away," it follows that those who live by the light and who hope for the future that is dawning must live according to that hope.

Thus, John's call to love is not a mere ethical call. John is not saying simply that, because love is good, we should love. He is saying that the old order is passing away. This old— and still present—order, which John calls "the world" or "the darkness," calls for a certain attitude and a certain type of action. But the new order, which he calls "the light," calls for a different type of life—what he calls "walking in the light."

> "Then I saw a new heaven and a new earth; for the first heaven and the first earth had passed away, and the sea was no more" (Rev. 21:1).

In the affirmation that "the world and its desire are passing away" we hear echoes of Revelation. In both there is a strong expectation for the end and fulfilment of history—what is usually called an "eschatological" expectation. Because of that expectation, Christians ought to live out of the future that is dawning. But there is also a marked contrast between the eschatology of First John and that of Revelation. As a commentator has put it:

> In affirming the passing of the world the author probably did not have in mind any cosmological eschatological catastrophe; this is not the disappearance of the first heaven and earth of Rev. 21:1, where a transformed new heaven and earth will replace the old. In 1 John's thought such vivid eschatological imagery has been transformed to become a way of expressing the utter incompatibility between the sphere that represents God's will and intention, and all that opposes it, as well as the complete certainty that, regardless of whatever might have been happening in society and to this community of believers, the opposition to God was irreversibly doomed.[13]

First John is about a coming new order, about the passing of the old, and in this sense it is very much like Revelation. But, in contrast to Revelation, in First John the emphasis lies on love of God and of one another—a love that expresses the hope of believers for what is to come.

John's readers would find baptismal overtones in much of what he has said so far: new life, cleansing, light, fellowship. Obviously, the letter is written to those who have been baptized. In that sacrament, they knew that they were cleansed from sin, they were illumined—that is, given light to know the truth—and joined both to Christ and to all other Christians. Going into the water they had joined the death of Christ, rising from the water they had joined the new risen life that he brings. His blood—his death—is the agent of their cleansing. It is also the blood of the new covenant, allowing them to enter into this new people of God. The letter is calling them to live out the meaning of their baptism. Baptism cleansed them from sin, and opened the way for forgiveness in the future. Baptism joined them to God, and they should live as those who did indeed have fellowship with God.

We too are baptized, and all that was said to these ancient Christians applies to us as well. Because we are related to God through Christ, and particularly because of the death of Christ—the blood that was shed for us—we have continued access to God's forgiveness when we confess our sins. We are to be truthful, and that truth includes the fact that we are sinful. Sin divides us from God and also from the community of believers. If we deny our sinfulness, then we are calling God a liar. Either God is a liar or we are. If the truth is in us, then we know that we are sinful and we also know that God is forgiving. Acting on that truth means confessing our sin, so that the just and faithful God will forgive us and let us continue walking in the light and having fellowship not only with God but also with one another. All of this is quite similar to the words of Jesus in John's Gospel: "I am the light of the world. Whoever follows me will never walk in darkness but will have the light of life" (Jn 8:12). Baptism engrafts us into the body of Christ, and when we follow him as true disciples, we will never walk in darkness. He remains our Advocate with the Father, keeping us in our fellowship with God.

There is an added thought at the end of 2:2. The saving power of the death of Christ is not simply for us. It is for the whole world. It is for that reason that the good news of Jesus Christ is to be proclaimed to everyone. God's love is for the whole world. Even those small groups of Christians in and around the Roman province of Asia, considered to be of no account by their pagan neighbors, have a message of upmost importance for those neighbors and for the entire world. They too can be forgiven for the deeds done in the darkness in which they live. They too can be given the light so that they can walk freely in companionship with God, with Christ, and with the Christians whom they now despise. God's love, which we have experienced and know is true, is also for them. Of course, if our lives belie our message, others have no reason to hear us. We must walk in the light in order to be able truly to proclaim that light to others.

CHAPTER 4

Abiding in Him in the Face of Opposition:
First John 2:18–3:3

This new section of the Epistle connects with the preceding by the theme of eschatology—of the end-time. We have just read that "the world and its desire are passing away," and now we are told that this is "the last hour"! As was stated in the introduction, the entire body of Johannine literature shares the view that the end has begun. While this seems to be the central theme in Revelation, it is mostly an undercurrent in the Gospel of John. First John had said nothing about it until 2:17; but now it comes to the foreground. This happens precisely at the point where John is about to begin talking about opponents against whom his readers must guard. In this, the eschatology of First John is similar to that of Revelation, for both draw a line between those who belong to the new order and those who do not; between those who remain firm and those who waver. Even without the violent imagery of Revelation, there is no doubt that First John envisions a struggle in which the forces of evil and untruth oppose God and

God's people.

The antichrist appears here as a central element in this eschatological struggle. It is interesting to note that, although most people think of the antichrist as a central theme in Revelation, the book does not even mention his name. Indeed, the word "antichrist" appears only in three verses in the entire New Testament: here, in First John 4:3, and in Second John 7. The antichrist is mentioned also in slightly later Christian literature from the same area that seems to have been the center of Johannine theology—for instance, the Epistle of Polycarp, bishop of Smyrna, two or three decades after the writing of First John. Both here and in 4:3, John refers to the antichrist as someone of whom his audience has heard, and therefore we may assume that it was a frequent theme of Christian teaching in the area. But one should also note that both here and in Second John 7 the notion that there will be a single antichrist is rejected, and we are told that there are multiple antichrists. This is one of many cases in which what people believe the Bible says is not exactly what it says. Indeed, throughout history, and even today, many have been convinced that the antichrist is someone in particular. But what John tells his readers is different. He tells them that they have heard of the antichrist—from whom, is not clear—but that there are many antichrists. Their presence is a sign that we are indeed in the last hour—or, as he put it in 2:17, that "the world and its desire are passing away."

Then John surprises us further by what he says about the origin of these antichrists. We tend to think that the antichrist is someone particularly evil, someone who persecutes the church or whose evil is blatant—a Nero, or a Hitler, or a Stalin. But according to John the antichrists have come out of the very community of faith. In verse 19, John is at pains to show that, although these people emerged from the community of faith, they were not truly of that community. His argument here is rather circular: they cannot have been really part of us, because had they been such, they would not have left us (v. 19).

However, what most interests John is not those whom he calls antichrists,

but the flock that has remained, whom he seeks to protect from the allure-
ment of the antichrists. The beginning of verse 20 sets the contrast quite
clearly: in verse 19, the repeated subject of every sentence is "they"—*they*
went, *they* did not belong to us, if *they* had belonged, *they* would have remained, *they* made it plain, none of
them—and then verse 20 opens with
"*but you.*"

These people whom John calls
"you" have something special: they
"have been anointed by the Holy
One," and they "have knowledge."
There is much debate about the exact meaning of this anointment, or
who is "the Holy One." Yet there is
no doubt that John has chosen the
word "anointed" quite purposefully.
What the Greek says is literally "you
have the anointment," and the word
for "anointment" is *chrisma*, which
is the same root from which Jesus
is called the Christ, the Anointed.
Thus, John is speaking of anti*christs*
and reminding Christians that they
have received the *chrisma*, for which
reason they belong to *Christ*, and
not to the anti*christs*. Their power
to resist the antichrists is in the
chrisma they have received. Using
the imagery of baptism as engrafting, one could say that, since these
"antichrists" were baptized, their
grafts did not take.

" … but you shall be for me a
priestly kingdom and a holy
nation. These are the words
that you shall speak to the
Israelites" (Ex 19:6).

"But you are a chosen race,
a royal priesthood, a holy
nation, God's own people, in
order that you may proclaim
the mighty acts of him who
called you out of darkness into
his marvelous light" (1 Peter
2:9).

" … and made us to be a kingdom, priests serving his God
and Father, to him be glory
and dominion forever and
ever. Amen" (Rev. 1:6).

" … you have made them to be
a kingdom and priests serving
our God, and they will reign
on earth" (Rev. 5:10).

Being *chrismated* or anointed was a very significant act in the ancient world, and particularly in the biblical tradition. Prophets and kings were anointed. Items devoted to the sacred service of God were anointed. Thus, having received the *chrisma* John's audience would know that they had been set apart for sacred service, and that they were a priestly people—something that had been promised to Israel of old (Ex. 19:6), and that the New Testament now declares to be true of believers in Christ (1 Peter 2:9; Rev. 1:6; 5:10).

The point of disagreement among interpreters has to do mostly with whether John is referring here to an actual anointing—and if so, what sort of anointing, and in what context it was performed. We know for certain that at some point in the second century baptism was accompanied by an anointment. Those who were joined to Christ in baptism were anointed as he was anointed—they were made *christs*, anointed ones, by virtue of the *Christ*, the anointed One. We have a reminder of this in the use of the term *christen*ing by which baptism is sometimes known. In ancient baptismal services, the newly baptized were anointed with oil on the forehead as a sign that they were part of the holy, priestly people of God. If this was already the practice in John's time, what he was telling his readers was akin to what is said today in many churches at the beginning of the Sunday service: "remember your baptism." They will not be led astray by the anti*christ* because they have received the *chrisma* of *Christ*.

And they have the power to resist because they also have "knowledge." While John does not specify the content of such knowledge, the implication is both that they have learned the basics of Christian teaching and that they know the One in whom they have believed—remember what was said in the previous section regarding the two parallel meanings of the verb "to know."

John then returns to his earlier contrast between truth and falsehood. The two cannot be mingled. Those who are in the truth cannot lie. And, in consequence, those who lie are not in the truth.

But here "lying" is not simply saying something that is not so. It is not any sort of fibbing. It is speaking untruth about the Truth, about Jesus. John is not moralizing about the evil of making up stories. He is trying to make sure that his readers do not listen to those whose teaching is erroneous. Nor is he referring to a relatively minor erroneous teaching. He is referring to the central issue of Christianity, the issue of who Jesus is. Thus, "the liar" in this context is "the one who denies that Jesus is the Christ," and who also "denies the Father and the Son."

The first of these "lies" has traditionally been understood as John's response to a certain Cerinthus. Although little is known about him, Cerinthus was a teacher who lived in Ephesus late in the first century or early in the second, who seems to have held that "Jesus" is the man, and "Christ" is the heavenly One who came upon Jesus at his baptism. Apparently the reasoning behind such teachings was that the heavenly being, the Christ, should not be subject to physical birth, suffering, and death. Whatever the teachings of Cerinthus may have been, Irenaeus—a Christian bishop who was a disciple of Polycarp of Smyrna, who in turn was said to have been a disciple of John—tells the story of an encounter in Ephesus between John and Cerinthus. Irenaeus reports having heard from Polycarp that once, when John learned that Cerinthus was in a bathhouse, he ran out of the building so as not to be under the same roof as one whom he called "the enemy of the truth."[14] Although more recently many interpreters have questioned the veracity of the story, the words in First John 2:22 would seem to refer, if not to Cerinthus himself, to someone who held similar doctrines. In that case, when the rest of verse 22, and all of 23, refer to those who deny the Son and the Father—the second lie—John is rejecting doctrines that, by denying that Jesus is the Christ, also deny that he is the Son, and in consequence also deny the Father.

Earlier, John has called those who say they have fellowship with God, but walk in the darkness, "liars" (1:6; 2:4), and has made it clear that walking in the light is loving others in need. Is he now referring to another sort of liar, whose lie is doctrinal rather than practical? While it is impossible to tell, it would seem not. The practical lie of those whom John criticizes for not loving others is connected with the doctrinal lie that John begins to attack here, and that will become clearer in chapter 4. John's point is precisely that what one does is not independent of what one believes. One affects the other, either confirming it or denying it. This is the point of the words of Bonhoeffer quoted above. First John never distinguishes between morally reprehensible behavior and doctrinal error. Although interpreters disagree on this point, it seems that those whom he criticizes, and against whose attraction he is trying to protect his readers, are people who teach false doctrine, and who also do not practice love for others.

Just a few years after the writing of this Epistle, Ignatius, a bishop of Antioch whose theology was profoundly shaped by the Johannine tradition, wrote seven letters on his way to martyrdom in Rome. In them he calls readers in various churches to reject doctrines that he considered pernicious, and which were rather similar to those attributed to Cerinthus. In one of those letters, referring to those whose theological opinions he is refuting, Ignatius declares that "They have no regard for love; no care for the widow, or the orphan, or the oppressed ... or the hungry, or the thirsty."[15] Ignatius, like John before him, is connecting false teaching or heresy with lack of love. Neither he nor John are saying what we hear so often today: "It doesn't matter what you believe, as long as you do what is right." Nor would they hold to the opposite view, that all that is important is what you believe. They would say that the two are interconnected, for the love of others is an expression of one's living—John would probably say "abiding"—in the love of God.

Over against the attraction of such doctrines, John exhorts his readers to "let what you heard in the beginning abide in you." This introduces the theme of abiding, which had appeared earlier, almost in passing, in 2:6, 14, and 24. This theme is typically Johannine, for the verb "to abide" appears in this letter more than anywhere else in the New Testament, and the other book in which it also appears several times is the Gospel of John. Although John has used this verb earlier in the Epistle, it is at this point that it comes to the foreground by sheer repetition. Note how often the verb "to abide" appears in the rest of chapter 2: three times in verse 24, twice in 27, and once again in verse 28. From this point on, this theme will recur, constantly reminding us of its importance. The word that the NRSV translates as "abiding" has also been translated as "indwelling," or as "remaining." Actually, the NRSV itself occasionally translates it as "remained"—for instance, in 1 Jn 2:19. The combination of these various possible translations gives us a fuller flavor of the meaning of the word. It means to dwell permanently or to live, as when we say "I live in Kansas." The word "abide" is somewhat archaic, but it expresses an essential idea in First John. In some older translations of the Bible, the words of the disciples to Jesus on the road to Emmaus are: "Abide with us. ..." The NRSV translates this as "Stay with us. . ." (Lk 24:29). The famous hymn, "Abide with Me" is based on these words. To abide means to continue, to remain, to dwell, to live in—as in John 15:4-8, where the NRSV translators felt it necessary to use the archaic words because "stay" did not convey the whole sense. The passage begins: "Abide in me as I abide in you." To "abide" has more of the sense of dwelling in, being a part of. To "stay" does not mean the same. As a command to a dog it clearly separates the speaker from the dog, if the dog is obedient. But when Jesus tells us to abide in him, it is to be a part of him as he is part of us. This goes back to the meaning of baptism as an engrafting into

"Abide in me as I abide in you. Just as the branch cannot bear fruit by itself unless it abides in the vine, neither can you unless you abide in me. ^{5}I am the vine, you are the branches. Those who abide in me and I in them bear much fruit, because apart from me you can do nothing. ^{6}Whoever does not abide in me is thrown away like a branch and withers; such branches are gathered, thrown into the fire, and burned. ^{7}If you abide in me, and my words abide in you, ask for whatever you wish, and it will be done for you. ^{8}My Father is glorified by this, that you bear much fruit and become my disciples" (Jn 15:4-8).

Christ, letting us dwell in him, and he in us.

Looking at the entire Epistle from the vantage point of this "abiding," we see that this is John's way of dealing with his central concern. Some people have left the community. They have not remained in the community. Now he is exhorting his readers not to follow these people. They are to remain in what they have received; they are to remain in the community. It is only by doing this that they remain in God, and God remains in them. John employs this theme of abiding as a bulwark against the attraction of the "liars" who teach false doctrine and who do not practice love.

As we study the passage further, we see that it is not always the same subject that abides, nor is the abode always the same. In the first two references in verse 24 to abiding, it is what they have been taught that should abide in John's readers. But then the third reference reverses the direction, for if the abiding that has been described in the earlier part is true—that is, if the truth abides in believers—then there is an abiding in the opposite direction, and it is now the believer who will abide in the Son and in the Father. In verse 27 there is a similar movement from one direction to the other, for first it is the anointing that abides in believers, and then it is these believers that will "abide in him." And in verse 28 it is again a matter of believers abiding in him.

This indicates that what John understands by "abiding" is a reciprocal relationship. When the truth of God abides in believers, they also abide in God—which reminds us of Paul's double usage, referring to believers as being "in Christ" and, reciprocally, to Christ as being in them.

Verse 29 seems to be disconnected from the rest of the discourse, and for this reason the NRSV places it as the beginning of a new paragraph that moves into chapter 3. Here the connection between who God is and who believers must be turns to the matter of righteousness, again in a sentence beginning with the conditional "if." If you know that God is righteous, you also know that those who are righteous are born of him. (Note the notion of being born of God, that appears also in the Fourth Gospel.) The word translated here as "righteous" also means "just" —as in 1:9, where we are told that God is faithful and "just." Thus, the righteousness to which John is referring is not only abiding by a code of clean conduct; it is also practicing justice, meeting the needs of those who are less fortunate—in a word, practicing love, for in God love and justice are one, and the same ought to be true of those who claim to be children of God. (Note that we have just used the word "abiding" in a different way, one that is not archaic—as in abiding by the law. In this context, it means more than following a law at this time, but that one lives by the law, that what is right and just is what one always is trying to do.)

The first three verses of chapter 3 return to the subject of eschatology, or of Christian hope, with which the present section began. This hope is based on a changed reality. According to John, it is by reason of God's love that believers can be called, and indeed already are, children of God. Note John's insistence that this is not only for the future. We are children of God *now*. It is possible that some of those whose teachings he rejects held that, just as according to them Jesus was made the Son of God at his baptism, so are believers made children of God at a future point—probably at death. But John will have none of that. We are children of God *now*!

Obviously, being children of God means that God, as a loving parent, takes care of believers. This is a common theme in the Gospels. But it means much more than that. In the ancient world, even more than today, people were often judged and classified according to who their father was. Occupations were often determined by the occupation of one's father. Social standing depended on the position of the head of the household. As we see throughout the Old Testament, nations were divided into clans according to their progenitors, and such clans were divided into families in the same way. We have a slight remnant of that today in the last names we are given, usually taken from our fathers. In such a context, to say that believers are children of God certainly means that God protects them like a loving parent; but it means much more. It means that who they are is defined by who their father is, God. It is difficult to imagine what this would mean for someone who had been brought up as a slave, or who was baseborn. I am no longer just a slave! I am no longer just a fishmonger! I am a child of the God most high! I am as much as the emperor, and even more!

But then, even though all of this may be true, things haven't changed much in the actual world. If I am a slave, my master still commands and exploits me. If I am a fishmonger, I still have to get up very early every morning to go buy my fish, and I still smell of fish. Furthermore, having become a Christian has not simplified matters; on the contrary, it has made them worse. People now look at me as if I were crazy. They exclude me from their associations and celebrations, because I will not worship their gods. How can it be that I am *now* a child of God?

John's answer is to point to the rejection Jesus himself suffered: "The reason the world does not know us is that it did not know him"—an assertion in which one hears echoes of the prologue to the Fourth Gospel. The world rejected the light, and still walks in darkness.

But there is another side to John's answer: eschatological hope. We are already children of God, and when he is revealed we too will be revealed in newness of life. We do not know—we cannot know—exactly what this means. John will not enter into the sort of discussion that the Corinthians seem to have found so attractive, and which led Paul to write to them about the final resurrection in First Corinthians 15. All that he says is that our present state is as children of God, and that what the future holds is even more than that! And then he does give a brief indication of what he expects that future life to be like: "we will be like him, for we will see him." In other words, any description or conception of life eternal will fall short, for it is life in God and in the likeness of God.

This entire section comes to an end in verse 3, which is both the conclusion of what precedes and a bridge into what follows. "All who have this hope in him purify themselves, just as he is pure." Hope is not just a matter of waiting for something to happen. Real hope practices for what is to come. A child who hopes to become like its parent imitates that parent even in its play. Likewise, those who hope to be like him who is pure must purify themselves; they must prepare for the time when the promise is fulfilled.

CHAPTER 5
Love as the Opposite of Sin: First John 3:4-24

We now come to a passage that includes what is perhaps the most baffling statement in the entire Epistle. This is the matter of the apparent sinlessness of believers, posed by the words in verse 6, "No one who abides in him sins; no one who sins has either seen him or known him"; and in verse 9: "Those who have been born of God do not sin." The difficulties are obvious. First of all, this contradicts what Christians have experienced through the ages, and what each one of us has experienced in his or her life. Good, sincere, faithful Christians do sin. Secondly, it contradicts what John himself has said earlier, when he states that "if anyone does sin, we have an advocate ... " (2:1). The apparent contradiction is so blatant that a number of scholars (particularly Rudolf Bultmann) have argued that what we have here is either written by a different author or at least taken from a different source. Such a solution, however, implies that whoever introduced this contradiction in the text was not sufficiently alert to notice it—which, given the cogency and consistency of the entire document, is highly unlikely.

John states that those who abide in Christ do not sin, and yet those who are in Christ and say they have no sin are liars. Both are true, however difficult this may be to state clearly. There is always room for growth in our abiding in Christ. That growth is what we term "sanctification," growth in holiness. Luther tried to say the same thing when he declared that Christians are one and the same time justified and sinners. In Paul's terms, in baptism we have died with Christ and we have been raised with him; we are living in the old creation and in the new creation at the same time. Hopefully, daily the old life has less power over us and the new life becomes stronger. It is God's love for us that lets us see where sin still has a hold on our lives, so that we can root it out, confess it and, through the power of the indwelling Christ, know that we are forgiven and strengthened for leading a more righteous, loving, and just life.

Quite clearly, what John is doing here is taking the incompatibility of sin and godliness to its final consequences. He is using the moral laxity of his opponents as an argument against them. We know that at a relatively early time there were those who claimed that, because they were of God, they were free from all law, and were free to do as they pleased. For this reason, John begins by linking sin with lawlessness. Those who claim that they are beyond the law are not free of sin. On the contrary, the very claim to be free of the law is the essence of sin. It is not just a matter of sin being lawlessness, but also of lawlessness being sin. Thus, the "everyone" to whom John refers here are the same ones who in 1:8 say that they have no sin. John's opponents claim that they have no sin, not because their life submits to the highest standards, but because they reject all standards—they practice *anomia*, lawlessness.

In contrast to such people stand John's readers who have remained firm: "*You* know that he was revealed to take away sins, and in him there is no sin." In other words, you know that the claims of these antinomians—opponents of the law—are false. They must be, for Jesus came to take away sins. Thus, the purpose of the entire argument is not, as would appear at first glance, to call readers to absolute sinlessness; it is rather to keep them from falling prey to those who feel free to sin egregiously, because they no longer hold to the law. This purpose is made clear in verse 7: "Little children, let no one deceive you." The deception comes from those who practice lawlessness as if it were not sin, and who apparently are calling others to similar lawlessness.

So that the "little children" may not be deceived, John goes back to his earlier argument, that the children of God are to be like God (see 3:3). He now expresses this in terms of righteousness: "Everyone who does what is right is righteous, just as he is righteous" (3:7). At this point, it is well to remember that the word translated here as "righteousness" also means justice. Thus, the verse could be translated as "everyone who does justice is just." Such a translation may be better, for in our common usage righteousness has to do more with personal rectitude, while justice has to do with interpersonal relations. As we have already stated, love and justice, properly understood, are not opposites, but are two sides of a single coin. To do justice is to practice love; and the proper practice of love leads to the highest level of justice. John is not calling his readers to personal rectitude. He is rather calling them to love. He is not just warning them against sin in general. He is warning them against people who claim that to sin is of no importance, and particularly that lovelessness or injustice are minor matters.

The conclusion of this argument about sin, justice, and truth is in the first half of verse 10, where John says that it is by doing right (justice) that the children of God are revealed, and that those who are not from God are also revealed in that they "do not love their brothers and sisters."

The reference to love at the end of verse 10 links the preceding to what follows. It shows that when John is speaking about sin he means primarily lack of love, and when he is speaking of righteousness or justice he means love for one another. In verse 11, there are echos of the very beginning of the letter when he declares that "this is the message you have heard from the beginning." This does not mean only that they heard things when they first heard the Gospel. It means also that this is a message "from the beginning," even before they heard, just as 1:1 refers to the very beginning of all things. Thus read, verse 11 stands in contrast with what John said in

3:8, that "the devil has been sinning from the beginning." The conflict is not between two opinions, or between two different understandings of how things are. The conflict is between the sin that the devil practiced from the beginning and the message that contradicted the devil, also from the beginning. And this eternal message is "that we should love one another."

The example of Cain in verse 12 then serves a double purpose. First, there is the obvious point that fratricide, or hate of brothers or sisters, is at the very heart of sin. But then the story of Cain also serves as an explanation of why "the world hates you." Cain killed his brother because his own deeds were evil, while his brother practiced justice. It is for the same reason that the world now hates believers.

Over against such attitudes, love is the mark of those who have passed "from death to life." Thus, the typically Johannine polarity between death and life is now joined with the polarity between love and hatred. And, just as there are no shades or gradations between death and life, John leaves no room for shades or gradations between love and hatred. John never speaks about loving a little bit. He speaks simply about love and hatred. Not to love—not to love radically—is to hate. There is love for brothers and sisters, and there is hatred for brothers and sisters. But there is nothing between the two. We would like to think that we could love others a little bit, or at least take a neutral stance and not hate them. But John's vocabulary seems to indicate that not loving is tantamount to hating. Such hatred may not be active and virulent, as when we set out to kill someone. But if it is not love it is un-love; it acts as if the other person did not exist, or were not worthy of our attention. And that John would call hatred!

What does John mean by love? He means simply what God has manifested in Jesus, whose example in this passage contrasts with the earlier reference to Cain. John says that "we know love" by the action of Jesus when "he laid down his life for us." Again, to "know" may have two different but interrelated meanings. On the one hand, one can know that something is true. On the other, one can know someone. To know one's parents—to experience their love and their values—is not the same as to know that one's parents are Mary and Bill. One does not exclude the other. But the highest sort of knowing is the first. It is to this sort of knowledge that John refers here. It is not just that we know what love is, although it certainly includes that. It is first and foremost that we know, that we encounter, that we experience love in Jesus' action of laying down his life for us.

This emphasis on the need to show love both in actions and in faith is common to the General Epistles. In some cases, these letters show that Paul's emphasis on faith sometimes was misunderstood as separable from actions, and these Epistles are righting the balance. Second Peter clearly states that: "There are some things [in Paul's letters] hard to understand, which the ignorant and unstable twist to their own destruction" (2 Peter 3:16). In James we find a similar sentiment: "Faith, by itself, if it has no works, is dead" (James 2:17). In John's terminology, to say that we have faith that God loves us is, if this does not result in love for others, a lie. First Peter declares that love for one another is so important, that even if a congregation is deficient in other ways, "love covers a multitude of sins" (1 Peter 4:8).

The assertion that Jesus laid down his life is typically Johannine, for in the New Testament it appears only in First John and in the Gospel of John. We tend to read it in the context of similar phrases that affirm that Jesus died for our sins—which undoubtedly is true. But in other Greek literature of the time it actually means to stake one's life on something. A friend lays down his life when he offers himself as a hostage in order to have his friend freed. A soldier lays down his life when he jumps forward in defense of a companion under attack. Thus, although when Jesus lay down his life this led to his death, John is not calling his readers to rush into death for others, or saying that their love will only be true if they actually die for others. He is saying rather that, just as Jesus took every risk, and even offered his life, for love of others, so must his followers put their lives on the line for the sake of others. The love that believers in Christ must have for one another knows no boundaries, just as Jesus in his love was willing to give up his life for us.

In verse 17 John begins to spell out what this means in concrete terms. Given our penchant for the heroic, we expect John to say that true love is best seen in heroic actions, such as actually dying for another or jumping in front of a rushing cart to save someone. Thus, we may be surprised to see that, instead of speaking of an ultimate heroic sacrifice, he speaks of sharing goods. But the truth is that too often lofty ideals or heroic goals are used to avoid faithfulness and commitment in what does not reach such levels of sacrifice. When we do not actually have a million dollars, it is easy to say, "if I had a million dollars I would give them to this cause," and then not to give the thousand that we do have. Likewise, it is easy to say that our love of God is such that we would be willing to suffer martyrdom—to lay down our lives—and at the same time not to show such love in our everyday decisions.

In this particular case, even after speaking of how Jesus laid down his life for us, and saying that believers must respond in kind, John turns to the sharing of material goods. This might seem to be a sharp descent from the lofty heights of laying down one's life. But in truth it is a more demanding call than simply saying that believers ought to be ready to lay down their lives for one another. There might not be many occasions when a believer would be called to lay down his or her life for another. But there certainly must have been many occasions when a believer had more than was necessary, and upon seeing another in need was called to help that other person. What John is then telling them is rather drastic: if they have what they do not need, and fail to share it with those who do not, they are not practicing love. Since there is no middle ground between love and hate—or un-love—, those who do not share with the needy hate them. And "all who hate a brother or sister are murderers" (v. 15)!

Love is not just a feeling. It is not simply a matter of saying "I love you." True love is manifested in action. And the love of God must be manifested in action towards God's children. To claim that the love of God "abides" in us, and at the same time to refuse to meet the needs of sisters and brothers whose wants we may supply, is to lie. To love "in truth and action" is contrasted with loving "in word or speech" (v. 18). Today we would say that one must not only talk the talk, but also walk the talk. Note the repetition of the word "truth" in verses 18-19. To love in truth is the proof "that we are from the truth" —or belong to the truth. Thus the theme continues, of the need to reject the false teachers who would call believers away from the community, who practice lawless sin, and who do not seek to meet the physical needs of others. Once again, these are not separate: it is those who fail to practice love who also fail to obey God, and also those who seek to tear the community apart by leading others astray.

In verses 19-21, John presents two possible attitudes or conditions. In one, our hearts condemn us; in the other, our hearts do not condemn us. Today we would probably say that our conscience condemns us or, in the opposite case, that we have nothing on our conscience. Significantly, John does not say, as many would today, that you are right with God only if your conscience does not condemn you. John rejects such a notion with what amounts to one of the most radical and least known expressions of the love and grace of God. Your heart or conscience may condemn you; but God is greater than your heart or your conscience, and knows everything. In other words, even those things that you wish you could hide from God you cannot hide. God knows them. And still God loves you.

According to John, the way we learn and experience this is by practicing love. Verse 19 says it quite clearly: by loving in truth and in action we know that we are from the truth, and this sustains us whenever our hearts condemn us. In other words, the practice of love helps us understand and experience the love of God, who does not condemn us even when our hearts do.

Then there is the opposite case, when our hearts do not condemn us—or, as we would say today, when we have a clear conscience. In such cases, "we have boldness before God." The word employed here is most often connected with open, frank, and free speech. To be bold is to say what is in one's mind. In the ancient world, this was not always considered good, and could even be dangerous. What one was able to say to another depended on the relative status of the two. Those who prided themselves on their democratic or republican systems of government held that one of the rights of citizens was the freedom to speak boldly—a right which obviously was not extended to slaves, freedmen, clients, and others who were considered inferior. In the early church, there would be few who had such a right. And certainly none who could speak boldly to the highest imperial authorities. But these Christians are being told that they have the right to speak boldly, not to their social superiors, or to the emperor, but to God! This may even have been expressed in worship. We know that shortly after the writing of this Epistle, and perhaps already at the time, Christians would kneel and bow their heads to pray every day, except on Sunday. Sunday was the day of their adoption. As heirs to the king, they had the right to speak to God face-to-face, boldly. It is impossible to tell whether such were the practices of the Johannine churches at the time. But whether it was expressed in this liturgical fashion or not, the Christian message was such that it allowed those who had been made children of God to approach God as a prince would approach a king, and not as a petitioner.

In the passage we are studying, petition is certainly at issue. Since the matter of God responding to the petitions of believers will surface again later in the Epistle (5:14-16) in ways that are parallel to the present passage, we will discuss it more fully in that context. Here, however, the emphasis is not on God granting us what we ask for as much as it is in our trusting God sufficiently to speak out in boldness, trusting God's love and grace. Actually, the phrase "because we obey his commandments and do what pleases him" should be understood as the reason both for receiving what we request and for speaking boldly. In this regard, note that the text says: "*we have boldness* before God, *and we receive* from him whatever we ask, because we obey his commandments and do what pleases him." Obeying God's commandments makes it possible both to ask with boldness and to receive with gratitude.

In verses 23-24 John tells us more about what he means by these commandments. At the time of the advent of Christianity, there were discussions about how many were the commandments of God. We can hear echoes of such discussions in the question posed to Jesus about which is the greatest of all the commandments (Mt 22:34-39; Mk 12:28-31). Now First John, after speaking of the "commandments"—in the plural—speaks of "his commandment," as a single one. The plural form will reappear in verse 24. But the combination of singular and plural conveys the impression that there is a single, central commandment that is John's main concern, and that he reads the others in the light of this one. And even then, the apparently single commandment is double: "that we should believe in the name of his Son Jesus Christ and love one another." This seems confusing, for one element of the commandment has to do primarily with matters of belief, and the other with matters of attitude and behavior. But this is precisely John's point: belief and behavior must go together. John has repeatedly said this in various ways. Anyone who claims to believe in God but does not love others is a liar. Now he links belief in Jesus Christ with love. As Christians, we are called to believe in Jesus *and* to love others. One without the other does not suffice, and turns out to be false. Then verse 24 repeats the statement, returning to the theme of abiding, which at this point has taken center stage in the Epistle.

Finally, John tells his readers that this abiding is confirmed "by the Spirit that he has given us." This is the first time that the Epistle refers to the Spirit. This is often understood in terms of "the testimony of the Spirit"—meaning that Christians know that they are saved because the Spirit attests to that within their own selves. There may be other passages to support this view; but this is far from the thrust of what John is saying here. First of all, he is not speaking of some inward knowledge an individual has. In this context, the issue is belief in Jesus and love of others. Thus, it is not so much that the Spirit tells us something in secret as it is that the gift of the Spirit allows us both to believe and to love.

Furthermore, it is not absolutely certain that what the NRSV translates as "the Spirit" is a reference to the Holy Spirit. Ancient Greek manuscripts were generally written entirely in capital letters, and therefore there is no way to know what is a proper noun and what is not. This means that the phrase can also be translated as "the spirit that he has given us." Later (4:6),

John will speak of "the spirit of truth and the spirit of error." It may well be that here he is referring to the first of these two. There is no doubt that such a spirit would still be a gift of the Spirit; but in this case the testimony we receive is not an inner assurance, but rather finding ourselves obeying the commandment—that is, believing and loving.

As we shall see, this reference to "the Spirit that he has given us" may well serve as a bridge joining this section of the Epistle to the rest.

CHAPTER 6
Testing the Spirits: First John 4:1-6

W hen John wrote or dictated his letter, he did not divide it into chapters and verses. This came much later, as people sought ways to be able to refer to specific portions of the Epistle—or of other texts. Since we often read the Bible a chapter at a time, we often miss connections that could help us understand what the text actually says. In this particular case, it may be well to try reading the end of chapter 3 as the beginning of the next section, and not only as the end of the earlier one. (In truth, given John's practice of linking thoughts, those words are most probably both the end of the previous section and the beginning of the next one.) We would then read: "And by this we know that he abides in us, by the Spirit that he has given us. Beloved, do not believe every spirit, but test the spirits to see whether they are from God." Thus read, the text refers to the existence of a multitude of "spirits," some from God and some not, and we know that Jesus abides in us by the sort of spirit that is ours.

As we read the passage, the first important point to note is that not all that is "spiritual" is good. Today there is in many churches a strong and healthy emphasis on spirituality. This is as it should be. But this must not be taken to imply that anything that is "spiritual" is necessarily good. According to John, there are spirits, and there are spirits. The task he here sets before his readers is the testing of the spirits, the discerning between those spirits that are from God and those that are not.

It makes little difference whether John understands such "spirits"—both positive and negative—as actual spiritual beings, or is rather using the term as we do when we say, for instance, "that's the spirit!" The purpose of the letter is not to inform us as to the existence or the nature of such beings. Its purpose is to show that there are true and false spirits—no matter whether they are invisible beings, or doctrines and attitudes. Most likely John is thinking in terms of such beings; but his message is neither diminished nor strengthened by their existence or not.

Apparently, testing the spirits is an urgent matter for John because he sees great danger in some of the "spirits" that are circulating at the time. Such spirits are being promoted by the "many false prophets that have gone out into the world." As we shall see, these prophets teach doctrines that John considers unacceptable and a contradiction of the Gospel itself. For that reason, here his emphasis will be almost entirely doctrinal. It will be a matter of what one believes—or rather, of what spirit one follows, of what one's spirit leads one to believe. But immediately, in the next section, John will return to the subject of love, thus showing once again that for him belief and behavior are closely interwoven. We have seen throughout this Epistle the combination of belief and action, although we often tend to separate them. But if the belief is "love," how can it not result in action? To say "God is love," and also to say that we believe that God abides in us and we in God, requires that this love manifest itself.

The touchstone that John proposes as a means to distinguish between those spirits that are from God and those that are not is what such spirits say about Jesus. On the positive side (v. 2), it is possible to know where the Spirit of God is acting (here the NRSV is probably justified in capitalizing

"Spirit") by what various spirits confess. Any spirit—or, we could say, any doctrine or attitude—that confesses that Jesus Christ is come in the flesh is of God. Here the emphasis lies on the word "flesh." There were in ancient times—as there are today—many who thought that to be truly "spiritual" meant to have nothing to do with material realities, and particularly with the flesh. For such people, the body is evil, and there is within each us, entrapped in that evil body, a spiritual reality that is good. If that is the case, then the purpose of life and of salvation is for the good spirit in us to escape from the evil, material body.

John would oppose such theories with all his strength. For one thing, they deny the doctrine of creation, which Israel held of old, and Christianity reaffirmed. All things were made by God, and all are essentially good. But even more, John would oppose such theories because they provide an excuse for not tending to the needs of others. One could do precisely what John so strongly condemns, claiming to believe in God and to love God, and yet doing nothing for a sister in need. One could even say to such a sister, "Go in peace, God loves you," while ignoring her hunger or her homelessness. Thus, while in this passage John seems to be talking only about doctrine, the matter of behavior—and particularly of love and its expression in concrete acts of love—is always just below the surface.

Such doctrines soon found expression among some Christians who believed that Jesus was indeed from God, but who then said that, since the flesh is part of the realm of evil, Jesus could not have come in the flesh. Jesus was a pure spirit. Perhaps he seemed to have flesh, to be a full human being; but this was mere appearance. Apparently one of the people who proposed such theories was John's contemporary Cerinthus, to whom we have already referred (and who, according to Ignatius of Antioch, not only taught false doctrine, but also refrained from practicing love).

It is against such people that John reaffirms the flesh of Jesus: "every spirit that confesses that Jesus Christ has come in the flesh is from God."

This is followed by its negative counterpart: "every spirit that does not confess Jesus is not from God." This could be no more than the reaffirmation, now in negative terms, of what John has just said. It is interesting to note that some ancient manuscripts say "every spirit that dissolves [or undoes] Jesus." If this reading is correct, then John is also referring to people who, like Cerinthus, distinguished between a human "Jesus" and a divine "Christ." By separating the two, the difficulties of the Incarnation seem to be resolved. But the truth is that what is important for Christianity is not that there is a Jesus and a Christ, but that Jesus is the Christ—and, as John would say, that Jesus Christ has come in the flesh.

John is quite harsh with those who hold the doctrines he rejects: "this is the spirit of the antichrist." The antichrist is not someone who openly attacks Christianity, or who commits horrendous crimes. The antichrist is this spirit that disguises itself as more "spiritual," and leads people away from the true confession, that Jesus Christ has come in the flesh.

By declaring that the antichrist is already in the world, John builds a bridge into the next three verses, which seek to strengthen readers against the attractions and the threats of the world. Here the polarity is between being "from the world" or "not from God" (v. 5), and being "from God"—a phrase that appears three times in these three verses. Here the theme is one of victory—"you are from God, and have conquered them." This is a typical Johannine emphasis. In the midst of all sorts of difficulties, usually despised and occasionally persecuted, those who believe in Jesus are conquerors. It appears in the Gospel of John: "In the world you face persecution. But take courage; I have conquered the world!" (Jn 16:33). And it is also a central theme in the Book of Revelation, where the faithful are repeatedly called "those who conquer," and where the entire plot leads to the final victory of God. First John will return to this in chapter 4. Here, he emphasizes first of all the power of the one who abides in the faithful: "the one who is in you is greater than the one who is in the world." And then he claims that those who will not listen to the Christian proclamation will not listen because they are "from the world"—and this apparently includes both unbelievers and those others who have left the community and now profess false teachings.

We live in a time when things "spiritual" are very popular, and John's words that we must test the spirits are very relevant to our day. Many people create their own form of spirituality, combining crystals, yoga, the beauty of nature, forms of meditation, vegetarianism, and whatever else comes to mind, including some elements of Christianity. Some of these practices may have a place in the life of a Christian, but the idea that we each form our own spirituality to suit us forgets that Christianity is a community of faith that guides us, that there is a "given" that is essential to the Christian. We have real news that has been proclaimed to us, and that news is Christ. It may be that in past centuries the church itself has done a poor job of teaching and leading the faithful to know what it is to abide in Christ. We may not experience love for one another in the congregation, or even have enough time together to care about one another. But the bottom line is that we do not make up our own spirituality, though it can be shaped by our own experiences. To abide in Christ and to have Christ abide in us means that we need to know quite specifically who Jesus Christ is, and what he tells us about God: namely, that God is love, and has come into our history to find us. Testing the spirits is an important part of maturing as a Christian.

CHAPTER 7
Love Is at the Heart of It All: First John 4:7-21

Now we turn to the section in the Epistle that has its most often quoted words: "God is love." Not surprisingly, this statement is of such importance for John that he expresses it twice: first in verse 8, and then again in verse 16. These words are certainly at the heart of the entire passage; and the passage itself is the heart of the entire Epistle. There are other themes that have appeared repeatedly throughout the Epistle—themes such as abiding, light, obeying the commandments, etc. But all of these are trumped by the theme of love. Indeed, the word "love"—both as a verb and as a noun—and derivatives such as "beloved"— appears 52 times in the Epistle, thus showing its importance. But of those 52 times, 29 appear in the section we are now studying: four in verse 7; two in verse 8; one in verse 9; three in verse 10; three in verse 11; two in verse 12; none in verses 13-15; and then again three in verse 16; one in verse 17; three in verse 18; two in verse 19; three in verse 20; and two in verse 21. It should also be noted that many interpreters have shown the parallelism between much of what is said here and Jesus' words in John 3:16, "for God so loved the world that ... "

The beginning of this passage surprises us, for in the previous section John has written some rather harsh words about those whom he considers a threat to the Christian community. Usually, as we have seen, John threads one passage with another by means of common themes which often appear at the end of a section and then again at the beginning of the next. Here, however, there is no such transition or connection—at least, not obviously, for when we look at the passage more closely, and consider it in the context of the entire Epistle we see that there is indeed a connection.

One connection is in the theme of being "from God." In the previous section, John has contrasted those who are "from God" with those who are "from the world." Now he invites his readers—whom he calls "beloved"—to love, and to do this because "love is from God." This is so much the case, that John surprises us by declaring that "anyone who loves is born of God and knows God." At first sight, this might seem to be a declaration that any love, no matter its object or its form, is from God, and that anyone who loves something or someone, no matter whom or how, knows God. There are those today who hold that anyone who feels or expresses any sort of love is expressing the equivalent of the Christian love of which John speaks here. There were in John's time religions that held that their gods were to be found and served in acts of eroticism such as temple prostitution and the like. This is certainly not what John means. He has earlier spoken of love for the world as an evil. Like every other word, "love" can be twisted to mean just about anything. John has made it abundantly clear that the love to which he is referring is indissolubly connected with God's love in Jesus Christ, and with obeying his commandments. John is addressing a Christian community, and therefore is speaking of Christian love—love born, as he will say in a moment, out of God's love for us. To expand the meaning of his words, as if all love of any kind were of God, is to twist his meaning. (Even so, apparently there were copyists who feared that John would be misunderstood, and therefore amended the phrase in verse 7, "everyone who loves is born of God," to "everyone who loves *God* is born of

God." Such an amendment is not necessary if we remember the insistence of the entire Epistle on the connection between love of God and obedience to the commandments.) Naturally, this is not to say that the natural love within families, the love of parents for children, the love between spouses, the love between friends, is evil. It is to say that, at its best, it is a reflection of the love of God, which is the love that was "in the beginning."

Verses 7 and 8 restate the connection that John has established repeatedly between love and belief, although it is in this case in terms of the knowledge of God. As often for John, there are here only two options: one either loves and knows God, or does not love and does not know God. There are no in-betweens here. The possibility of knowing God and still not loving is excluded. And so is the possibility of loving without knowing God.

The exclusion of this second possibility might surprise us, who are quite comfortable with the notion that if one is a believer one should love, but may feel awkward with the counterpart in John's words, which imply that in order to love one must be a believer! Yet, this is precisely what John means. He makes this quite clear in verses 9 and 10, where he bases his understanding of love in what God has done in sending God's son as an "atoning sacrifice for our sins." In other words, John is not referring to just any kind of love. He is referring to the love of God as "revealed among us in this way." He does not say that such love has not been revealed elsewhere. But he is writing to members of the Christian community, and what is of uppermost importance to them is to know that the love John is speaking about is no less than the love of God. This is the prototype of love. At this point we are subtly reminded of what John said earlier, that love is laying down one's life for another, as Jesus did.

Then, in verse 11, John surprises his original readers as well as us. We would expect him to say that, since God has loved us in this self-giving manner, we ought to respond by loving God. That is true without a doubt. But, instead of drawing this obvious conclusion, John says that our response to God's love ought to be to love others! This twist in the argument then leads to the apparent shift in verse 12, where John introduces the invisibility of God. Within the context of what John is saying, this is not primarily a declaration about how God is; it is rather a way of telling readers that, since this God who has so loved us is invisible, and therefore our love to him cannot be expressed in the same actions, we ought to respond to the love of God, whom we cannot see, by loving others whom we can see.

Then, in verse 13, John seems to leave aside the subject of love. Readers may have noted that when we listed the many times that the word "love" appears in this entire passage, we listed no such appearances in verses 13-15. Thus, at first reading it would seem that John has strayed from the subject of love, to which he will return in verse 16. But there is much more than that in this apparent digression. After all the positive words about love, John is linking this to what he said before about the testing of the spirits, and the importance of confessing "that Jesus Christ has come in the flesh" (v. 4:2, and similar words in 4:3). As throughout the Epistle, his message is both about love and about belief; or rather, his message is about how each of these two requires the other. In 4:1-6 the emphasis lay on correct confession, on belief in Jesus and on who Jesus is. In 4:7-12 the emphasis has shifted to the matter of love, about which John has written words that amount to poetic prose. He will return to that emphasis in 4:16. But before he does that he wishes to entwine love and belief in such a way that no one will be able to separate them. This he does by introducing in the middle of his words about love these three verses that remind the reader of what was said before regarding proper belief.

This is subtly done by beginning this apparent digression with the same words that introduced the previous section on testing the spirits. There he said: "by this we know that he abides in us, by the Spirit that he has given us" (3:24). Here he says: "By this we know that we abide in him and him in us, because he has given us of his Spirit" (4:13). The theme of abiding, which is at the center of these three verses, also harkens back to previous sections in the letter. But the most obvious link, where the connection in unmistakable, is in the statement of belief of those in whom God abides: "those who confess that Jesus is the Son of God" (v. 15).

In short, this apparent digression simply reasserts John's central thesis: belief in Jesus and love of God and of others go together.

Then, in verse 16, John returns to the subject of love by connecting it with belief in the loving actions of God. Confessing Jesus Christ and abiding in God includes believing the unbelievable "love that God has for us." This is because, as John has already said and now repeats, "God is love." Here again we find the reciprocity of love and of abiding: On the one hand, God is love; on the other, believers are to love. On the one hand, those who love abide in God; on the other, God abides in them.

In verse 17 John begins to deal with love at its highest, that is, "love [that] has been perfected." Our immediate inclination is to understand this in terms of what John Wesley understood by being "perfected in love." In Wesley's usage, this meant that Christian perfection does not consist in not doing this or that, but simply in doing all things out of love. However, here the Epistle is not referring directly to such perfection. What the NRSV translates as "perfected" can also be translated as "reaching its goal." It is not so much a matter of love being flawless, as we usually understand perfection, but rather of love being brought to its goal, producing its intended results, and in this sense being fulfilled or completed.

Significantly, in verse 17, as this love is brought to its ultimate goal, John does not say that this happens *in* us, but *among* us. There is no room here for the individualism that is so prevalent in our culture, and even in our understanding of Christianity. As has already been noted, this Epistle employs the plural "we" and "you"—in its plural form, as in "ye"—almost exclusively. The only uses of the singular "I" are those in which John refers to himself. Up to this point, however, the use of the plural "you" and "we" could be understood as simply a form of addressing individuals collectively. For instance, to say that God abides "in us" could mean that God abides in each believer. But to say that love has been perfected "among us" means that such perfection is attained only collectively. The "beloved community" of which Martin Luther King and so many others have spoken so eloquently is not just a gathering of individuals who are beloved. While individuals are certainly loved, it is the *community* that is beloved, and its members are loved precisely as members of it. Thus, by affirming that the perfection or fulfillment of love takes place "among us," John is making it clear that it is not a matter of each one of us being loved by God, and then coming together to express that love, but rather of our being part of a community that is beloved of God, and being loved precisely because we are part of this community.

It is interesting that in classic monastic life the two great virtues have always been love and humility. Both of these virtues have to be learned and practiced in community. Individuals can claim to be truly loving and humble as long as they are alone or with agreeable people. But should they be in the company of a difficult person or of someone who does not respect them, their lack of these qualities will become apparent. Love requires others, as does humility. Within the Christian community there is to be love for one another because all are part of the same body. The church is not a social club of those whom we find compatible. Paul writes that we are to "Welcome one another, therefore, just as Christ has welcomed you, for the glory of God" (Rom. 15:7). The church is not a community we have created, but one into which Christ has invited those whom he wishes. We are to love those whom Christ has loved. It is for this reason the church must exist in the form of groups that meet together, face-to-face, over a period of time. Love is difficult to express if we only watch a service on television or meet on the Internet. Love requires physical presence at some point. For John, the issue is what happens when we gather and some members have needs that others can fulfill. In many of our own congregations, we are often hesitant to express financial needs, or else we are divided by denomination so that most members are of the same economic level. To the degree that these things are true, we are hampered in experiencing the kind of community of love John expects.

Although First John never uses the term "church" (which does appear in Third John), the concept is at the very heart of his theology. He is writing in part out of his concern that the church will be divided as a result of the false teaching that he is rejecting. Or, more precisely, he is writing to prevent his readers from leaving the church, the beloved community of faith, seeking God elsewhere. John would probably have a hard time with the notion that the church can be divided. If the church is the beloved community, there can only be one church. Members of that community may not like each other. They may disagree on many points. But if they are followers of Christ they are members of a single community. As a friend of ours put it, the church is the bride of Christ, and Christ has a bride, not a harem! In a more traditional note, Cyprian of Carthage (third century) declared that one can only have God as a father if one has the church as a mother. We may dislike such a statement, because it has often been used by particular ecclesiastical bodies to declare that there is no salvation outside of them. But what Cyprian says is true, and fully agrees with John's theology: the "beloved" are such as part of the beloved community, and not on their own. Love is fulfilled, not in them individually, but among them as a community.

As we continue reading, we may be surprised that John brings in the subject of judgment. Why speak of such a fearful subject in the middle of what is almost an ode to love? Precisely because love takes the teeth out of the fear of judgment. In this, this Epistle is surprisingly similar to the Book of Revelation, even though in our minds the two are so different. Although Revelation speaks about judgment in terrifying terms, its message is not one of fear, but of trust, victory, and joy. That book is not addressed to those who would have to fear the judgment. Rather, it is addressed to people who were hard pressed by society around them, for whom the future as that society understood it held no hope. To them, the book says that there is indeed hope, and that they have no cause to fear the evils that are about to come upon the world. We find it difficult to read the Book of Revelation as it was intended because we are not hard pressed as those early Christians were, because we are not excluded from this world that according to Revelation will be judged, and probably because our investment in that world is too high, and we fear its demise. But the first readers of Revelation would have seen in it a book of joy, telling them that they had no reason to fear the judgment to come.

The same is true of the First Epistle of John. John does not avoid the subject of judgment. God is just, and therefore judgment is to be expected. But, according to both the Epistle and the Book of Revelation, judgment is not to be feared, because love has been perfected among us. The fulfilment of love, its completion, is in the manner we look at the future. The community that knows that God loves does not despair, because it already knows the judge, and knows that this judge, who is love, has loved it to such an extent as to send his Son to suffer out of love for it. This community does not wait for an unknown one, but for the one whose love it has known in Jesus Christ.

And this is not only for the future. John refers to the present when he says that "as he is, so are we in this world." He has earlier said that the antichrist is already in this world (4:3). He now adds that so is God. If the antichrist is in this world, thus making life difficult for the community of faith—not only by direct opposition, but also by drawing people away from the community—so is God already present in the world, loving this community which the antichrist seeks to undo. Thus, although the love of which John speaks finds its completion, its goal, in the future, it is love already active and already present. As a commentator has put it,

> For 1 John Jesus' significance is not determined by his life or death in the past, nor by any position with God in the heavenly realm, nor yet by the hope of his future return; Jesus belongs to the present, to the here as well as to the now; his story is their story and he models for them the true meaning of their life.[16]

This does not mean that eschatological hope is of no significance. It means that such hope is also for the present life, for the Jesus whom Christians expect is also the one whom they have seen in the past, and the one who is now already in the world, working out his eternal purposes of love.

All of this helps us understand the often quoted words, "There is no fear in love, but perfect love casts out fear." These words are used most often in wedding ceremonies, or in the renewal of marital vows, as an indication that when two people truly love each other there is trust. This may be a proper use, but only if we remember that true conjugal love is not just something that two people have for each other, but is rather an expression of the true love of which John is speaking—a love revealed in God's giving of God's Son. It is not just a matter of two people loving one another, and therefore trusting one another; it is also a matter of two people who know that ultimately they have nothing to fear, because God is love.

In its fuller context, the assertion that "perfect love casts out fear" has an eschatological point of reference. When love reaches its goal, when it is completed, all fear is gone; and this is particularly true of the fear of judgment, for the judge has befriended us in love. This becomes clear as one reads the rest of verse 18: "for fear has to do with punishment, and whoever fears has not reached perfection in love."

In the very brief verse 19 John offers a crucial corrective to any who would turn love into a meritorious act—or, in more traditional terms, into a work meriting salvation. "We love because he [God] first loved us." Too often we think exactly the opposite, that if we love enough God will love us. There is always that danger when one speaks, as John does, of the "commandment of love." For many of us, a commandment is something we must do even if we would rather not. And it is true that quite often commandments remind us that something we are about to do—or something we have done—goes against the will of God. But a commandment is much more than that. A commandment is an expression of God's love for us. It is what God tells us to do, not out of some arbitrary decision, but because God knows what is best for us—as individuals and as a community. But here John reminds us that the ox must go before the cart. What is first is not our love, which then induces God's love for us. What is first—or, to use a Johannine phrase, "from the beginning"—is God's love for us, which in return calls for our love for God and for others. God's love for us is prior to, and independent of, our love for God. Love is not a meritorious act which God repays by loving us.

Love is an act of grace to which we respond by being imitators of the God who first loved us.

The last two verses of this section (vv. 20 and 21) repeat and summarize much of what John has already said. This includes such items as: 1) the epithet of "liars" for those who claim to love God but do not love a sister or a brother; 2) the contrast between God, who cannot be seen, and others who can be seen, and the need therefore to love the latter; and 3) the summary of the commandment as love for others.

The assertion that "God is love" (4:8, 16) deserves fuller attention. It clearly does not mean that any form of love is divine—which has been made abundantly clear above. But when we reduce it to the principle that God loves us, we probably miss some of its full meaning. First of all, we must remember that God is the creator of all things, and that therefore God loves all things. While there is certainly something special about the human creature, we are part of creation. God's love for us does not preclude nor diminish God's love for all creatures. Therefore, it would seem that we could say, extending John's words in ways that reflect some of the challenges of today, that whosoever claims to love God, and even to love brothers and sisters, but does not love the rest of creation, does not truly love God. The experience of God's love in redemption, to which John attests in 4:10, must lead us to care not only for others like ourselves, but also for those creatures whom many would harm out of greed or mere complacency.

Then there is another dimension to the assertion that "God is love." Over the centuries Christian thinkers have wondered what the assertion that God is love means, not just for us and for creation, but for God's own self. One cannot love in absolute solitude. Love requires an object, an other who is loved. How, then, can God be love, when there is none other besides God? Is the phrase simply a hyperbole, an overstatement making it appear that indeed love is eternally with God? Or is there a deeper sense in which love is indeed eternally in God? In the Gospel of John, we are told that "in the beginning was the Word, and the Word was with God, and the Word was God" (Jn 1:1). This does not deny the fundamental Judeo-Christian doctrine that there is only one God, for monotheism is absolutely non-negotiable. But it may well lead us to reconsider the meaning of the "mono" (one) in "monotheism." For us, oneness means aloneness. But God's unique oneness is such that it includes community within God's very self. And this community is such that it is absolutely one. In other words, in God both oneness and community exist in the highest degree—so high a degree, that the two are one. This is what is actually meant by the doctrine of the Trinity—not some mumbo-jumbo about three and one, but the fundamental truth that perfect oneness involves perfect community, and vice versa. God is love, because at its very heart the Godhead is a community of love.

This in turn implies that the "beloved community" is not just something we are called to create. It is not just a dream. It is the best way to speak of the God who is at once Source, Word, and Spirit—or, in more traditional terms, Father, Son, and Holy Spirit. The beloved community already exists. That is what God is. God is love because God is the absolute community of love. In seeking to create among us a beloved community, we are being nothing less than imitators of God. It is in this community—and only in such a community—that we can experience the astonishing fact that God is love!

Our community and the beloved community of the Godhead are not two totally separate communities. All the language about "abiding," along with words about the gift of the Spirit to us, imply that our human, gathered community of love is actually participating in that beloved community that is God. We, as the church, are part of the body of Christ, the incarnate second person of the Trinity. As such, we have been invited into this original beloved community that has been from the beginning. We have been given a foretaste of the coming kingdom in our life as the church here and now, but our love still needs to grow until it casts out all sin, all false loves in this world.

Chapter 8

A Concluding Summary: First John 5:1-21

Chapter 5 is essentially composed of several sections, each summarizing something that has been said before, but often adding a new dimension. The first such section includes verses 1 to 5. As was to be expected, its central theme is love. And, as throughout the Epistle, this theme is entwined with others: the belief that Jesus is the Christ, the experience of being born of God, obedience to the commandments as a sign of life, and the victory that belongs to those who believe and obey the commandments.

The first verse relates belief with love in a way that is new and yet parallel to what has been said before. The argument is essentially that believers in Christ are born of God, and that, since "everyone who loves the parent loves the child," believers must love one another. Also, although there is no reference here to Jesus as the Son of God, the implication is clear that the love to which John is referring, which extends to all who are born of the same parent, extends to Jesus as well as to all who believe in him. Verse 2 simply repeats what has been said before, that loving God and obeying God's commandments is a sign of being born of God. The reason why this is so is that loving God is tantamount to obeying the commandments. Since John has repeatedly presented love as the essence of the commandments, this is another way of saying what he has repeatedly affirmed, that it is impossible to love God and not love one's sisters and brothers—in the context of this paragraph, those who are born of the same parent.

Precisely because of this connection between love and the commandments, the latter are not burdensome. It is not a matter of doing what God commands simply because God says so, but rather that, because one loves God, one wishes to do what God also wishes. From this, John moves to another theme that he has addressed earlier: victory. We have already indicated that this is a typically Johannine theme, appearing not only here, but also in the Gospel of John and in Revelation. Finally, this section of five verses concludes as it began, with the importance of believing in Jesus (in v. 1, as "the Christ", and here, in v. 5, as "the Son of God"). By thus ending where he began, John has created a structure that is like a sandwich, with the two slices of bread being the confession of Jesus as the Christ, the Son of God, and the center being love—love as obedience to the commandments and as leading to victory over the world.

The next subsection, verses 6-12, is much more complex and even obscure in its meaning, for here John introduces ideas that have not appeared earlier in his letter—at least, not in the same way. The passage is difficult to interpret, since John does not explain what he means by "the water and the blood"—words that are repeated in the passage, and to which the Spirit is eventually added. Apparently in an effort to deal with the obscurity of the passage, and certainly trying to work the doctrine of the Trinity into it, some copyists added in verse 7 words that do not appear in the most ancient manuscripts. This is why there is a marked difference between the King James Version, which includes that addition, and the NRSV, which is based on the older manuscripts. The addition may be found in a footnote in the NRSV, and its insertion would result in the following version, in which the addition has been put in brackets: "There are three that testify [in heaven, the Father, the Word, and the Holy Spirit, and these three are one. And there are three that testify on earth]: the Spirit and the water and the blood, and these three agree." Since the words between brackets were clearly not part of the original Epistle, we shall not discuss them here, although readers might wish to know why they appear in some Bibles and not in others.

If we then look carefully at verses 6-12, we note that the entire passage centers on Jesus Christ, and on the matter of who he is. That much is clear, and to it we shall return. What is not clear is what John means by water and blood. Many scholars and interpreters feel that John is using phrases known to his readers, but not to us, and that therefore their meaning simply cannot be recovered. It is as if someone two thousand years from now were to read a document from the year 2008, and find in it, without any further explanation, the words, "Yes, we can." That future reader would understand the meaning of each of those words, but would find it impossible to know why they suddenly appear in the document, or what their meaning was to readers in 2008. Other interpreters, however, offer a variety of views, usually being careful not to claim that they fully understand what John has in mind in writing these words. And, to complicate matters, there is the question of the relationship between what John says here and what the Gospel of John says, that at the crucifixion of Jesus, "one of the soldiers pierced his side with a spear, and at once blood and water came out" (Jn 19:34).

One possibility is that John is rejecting the views of those who, because they deemed matter to be evil, claimed that Jesus did not have a real body, and that he was not truly born. Others held that Jesus was the human who was born of Mary, but that Christ did not come upon Jesus until his baptism, where he was declared to be the Son of God. It may well be that John stresses "the water and the blood" as a means to counteract such notions. In this case, coming "by water and blood" may be a very physical way of referring to birth, and therefore rejecting the notion that Jesus was not born as other humans are born, with all the materiality involved in birth itself. John then declares further that Jesus did not come by water alone, but by both water and blood. This could be a way of rejecting the notion that the Son of God came only at his baptism—that is, by the water—and a way of insisting on his coming as the Son of God from the very beginning of his human life—by the water and the blood. Or, water may refer to his birth, and blood to his death. The sentence that follows, that "the Spirit is the one that testifies," may well mean that what the Spirit does at the baptism of Jesus is to testify as to who Jesus is, and not—as John's opponents would claim—to make him Son of God. Then, when it comes to who Jesus is—both fully human and the Son of God by nature, from his very birth—there are three that testify: "the Spirit, and the water, and the blood." And John seals the matter by declaring that "these three agree."

All of this was done by divine agency, and therefore this testimony, which is not a purely human declaration, but "the testimony of God that he has testified to his Son," is to be believed, and the human theories as to how Jesus was born—or not born—and about his becoming the Son of God at his baptism are void.

Another possibility, which does not exclude the former, is that here John is turning to the liturgical setting in which his letter is to be read. As was pointed out in the Introduction, this letter was most likely written to be read at a gathering of the community for worship. During the first part of such gatherings, Scripture was read and commented upon. At first, this was obviously the Hebrew Scriptures—for at the time there was no New Testament. During this first period of gathering, letters and communication from other churches and church leaders were also read. It was through this repeated reading, and through a process of selection as to what documents should be read in worship, that the New Testament was eventually formed. At the time when John is writing, his letter would be read in the worship service, to be followed by the second part of the service, which was the celebration of communion. Among other Johannine literature, there is no doubt that Revelation was written to be read in such a setting, for much of its last chapter uses words that were used in communion. The Fourth Gospel may well have been written so that sections of it could be read in the worship of the church, in preparation for communion. In the case of the First Epistle of John, there is no reference to communion, and very little to the worship of the church. But now, at the end of the letter, John begins to turn the attention of his readers to what will follow, the celebration of communion. For the early church, there were two central events through which their Lord came to believers, baptism and communion—the water and the blood. Through these two, as well as through the life of the church, the Spirit is present in the church. Thus the Spirit is the one who testifies; but the water—baptism—and the blood—communion—also testify. If this is the meaning of water and blood, it would also indicate that when the Gospel of John declares that "water and blood" came out of Jesus' wounded side, this is a reference to both baptism and communion flowing from the death of Jesus.

In any case, the difficulties connected with the exact meaning of water and blood should not obscure the central thrust of the passage, which is the declaration as to who Jesus is. It is he whom the church confesses, and it is in response to the love of God manifested in him that the church in turn practices love. Once again, this connection between confessing the truth and doing the truth, between believing and acting, is central to the entire Epistle.

Those who believe accept God's testimony, attested by the Spirit, by water, and by blood. Those who do not believe reject that witness, and thus make God a liar. This assertion can be easily understood by thinking of a court of law. If the testimony of a witness is rejected, this is tantamount to declaring the witness to be a liar. Likewise, in rejecting God's testimony, those who do not believe are making God into a liar.

All of this then leads full circle to other themes that are central in earlier sections of the Epistle, but had not been mentioned for some time. God's witness concerning God's Son is also that life is in the Son, and that therefore those who have the Son have eternal life, while those who do not have him do not have such life.

According to his own statement in verse 13, this is John's purpose in writing, to tell his readers that they who believe in the Son also have eternal life. But, as was pointed out earlier, John is a believer writing to believers. He is not only trying to tell them that there is life in the Son. He is also insisting that in this life there must be both confession and action; that those who declare that they love God must show this in love for others.

Immediately after this reference to eternal life, John returns to another theme that has appeared earlier in his letter, boldness. This is the courage to speak one's mind. In many settings, "boldness" is not a good trait, for it implies tactlessness and can easily turn into offensiveness. Not so in this setting, because John is not speaking about being bold before others, but rather about being bold before God! If boldness towards others may prove offensive, boldness towards a king or ruler may prove deadly! The commonly used phrase, "to speak truth to power," is not always easy to follow; and in some circumstances, particularly when there is great inequality between the speaker and the power, it may have dire consequences. But here John declares that Christians have the right to speak to the highest power of all with boldness! This is so, because we know that the Ruler of all is not a despot who demands slavish submission. The Ruler of all, John's God, is love.

Furthermore, this boldness is grounded in the conviction that, if we ask anything according to God's will, God will hear, and "we know that we have obtained the requests made of him." John has already said that "we have boldness before God; and we receive from him whatever we ask, because we obey his commandments and do what pleases him" (3:21-22). The meaning of this is not that, if we obey God's commandments, God will reward us with whatever we ask. There are many today who take these words in that sense, and therefore claim that, if you are good, pray regularly, attend church, do not murder, or steal, or commit adultery, God will reward you by giving you a car of the latest model, or the job you want, or whatever else your heart desires. But this is not what John is saying. John is basing the boldness of the petition on the premise that the petitioner obeys the commandments by loving God and neighbor, and this obedience is also part of the petition itself. In other words, those who love God will ask for what God wishes.

They will not ask out of hatred, or out of greed, but out of love. And out of love God will respond to them, granting them all that is in accordance with God's loving purposes.

On the other hand, love does not mean the total obliteration of the self. Love does not mean simply to say, "yes, my dear, as you wish." Love requires the freedom to be oneself, to express one's preferences and opinions, and then to be ready to accept the other's response to such expressions. Christian boldness in prayer may well follow the example of Jesus' prayer in the garden: "Father, if it is possible ... ; but let your will be done." Whoever prays in this fashion will have what she or he asks, that God take into account one's will, but that in the end God's will be done.

Verses 16-17 have been the subject of much debate throughout the history of the church. Here again John introduces notions that he has not mentioned previously, and does little to explain them. These are the notion of "mortal sin" and "sin that is not mortal." As we have seen in the earlier part of the Epistle, John has to struggle with the tension between the purity to be expected of those born from God and the actual reality of the church, where sin is still present. Thus, after declaring that "if we say that we have no sin, we deceive ourselves" (1:8), he says that "no one who abides in him sins" (3:6). To say that believers do not sin would be patently untrue. To say that this is of no consequence would undermine the very notion of being born from God and into a new life. John needs to say that sin—any sin—is a very serious matter; and yet he has to affirm also the forgiving love of God. Now, at the end of his letter, he faces the same issue once again. But in this case he does so by speaking of sin that is mortal and sin that is not.

Throughout its history, the church has had to struggle with the tension between its message of love and forgiveness and its own holiness and purity. The church cannot simply say that all sin is of such consequence that those who commit them are forever cut off from God's grace. Nor can it say that, since God is in the business of forgiving, sin is ultimately of no consequence. The result has been a series of attempts to distinguish between those sins that Christians generally commit, for which they will be forgiven if they confess, and those other sins that are so egregious that they are unforgivable, or at least require long periods of penance before they can be forgiven. At some point, apparently early in the second century, Christians generally held that the most egregious sins were apostasy, homicide, and fornication. But at the same time they had to struggle with the cases of those who fell into one of these sins and then asked to be readmitted into the communion of the church. The general response of the church was not to make light of such sins, but still to allow for the forgiveness of those who had committed them and sincerely repented—a sincerity that would often require years and decades of repentance before one was readmitted into the communion of the church. Some held that, if one sinned after baptism, the only recourse left was the "second baptism" of martyrdom.

As time went by, there were formal classifications of sin, till finally the distinction was made between "mortal sin" (pride, covetousness, lust, envy, gluttony, anger, and sloth) and "venial sin." John would have found this distinction scandalous, for he would never have considered any sin "venial." All sin is an egregious rebellion and attack on the majesty and love of God. We should note that the later distinction betwen "mortal" and "venial" sin is all about attitudes and motives, while John is concerned about actions. It may be helpful to try to nip sin in the bud by stressing the attitudes that lead to sin, but John is concerned that the hungry be fed. It may well be that as we engage in actions of love our attitudes will change.

Still, John does make a distinction. For him some sin is "mortal"—as the NRSV translates what would literally mean "leading into death"—and some is not. Do we have here the first seeds of the distinctions that would later come to full bloom? Probably yes. But it should be pointed out that most likely what distinguishes "mortal sin" from that which is "not mortal" is not so much its moral enormity, but the manner in which it breaks the life of the community of love which John sees the church to be. The ones who have been the object of his most stringent attacks in the rest of the Epistle are not those who break the moral codes, but rather those who break the community. Those whose false teachings lead people away from the community he calls antichrists. Those who will not come to the aid of a sister or brother in need he calls murderers. Thus, the sin that leads to death is the sin that breaks the community, for eternal life is to be found in the community that receives it from Jesus. To break away from the community is to break away from Jesus and to break away from life. This is therefore sin that leads into death—or, as the NRSV says, mortal sin.

This is why John urges prayer for those whose sin is not mortal. If one sees "a brother or sister" sinning, one should pray for that person, whom God will restore to life—that is, to the community of those whose sin has been washed away by Jesus. But then there are others—John does not call them brothers or sisters—whose sin is unto death. This is so, not because it is morally more reprehensible, nor even because they repeatedly fall into it, but because it is sin that severs them from the community of life. Finally, John makes it clear that the fact that sin that is not mortal will be forgiven does not mean that one should make light of sin: "All wrongdoing is sin, but there is sin that is not mortal" (v. 17).

In verse 18 John winds up his letter with three parallel sentences, each beginning with the words "we know that." These three sentences summarize much of what the entire Epistle says. The first (v. 18) is an affirmation of protection from sin. Here again John states that "those who are born of God do not sin"—an assertion whose absoluteness John himself has denied by inviting believers to confess their sins. But now he relates this to another one—Jesus—who was "born of God" in a different way. Those who are born of God are protected by the One who was born of God. It is as children of the same parent that Christians look at Jesus. And it is as an elder brother that Jesus looks over his followers and protects them from "the evil one." The second affirmation is the background of the first, for it affirms two points that are at the foundation of the first: First, that we are God's children. Second, that "the whole world lies under the power of the evil one." Finally, the third "we know" sentence is a summary of the gospel as John understands it. It presents a concatenation of facts that Christians know, not as separate bits of information, but as one single reality: That the Son of God has come. That he has done this to give us understanding. That this understanding is so that we may know him. That he is true. That we are in him who is true. That this is Jesus Christ, the Son of God. That Jesus Christ is "true God and eternal life."

The letter ends with a final admonition: "Little children, keep yourselves from idols"—which comes as a surprise to us, since John has said very little about idolatry.

Chapter 9
Truth and Love: Second John

In contrast to First John, Second John does follow the format of a letter. As was typical of the time, it begins by stating who is writing to whom: "The elder to the elect lady and her children." But, unlike other letters, the actual names of the writer and the recipients are not given. Who is "the elder," and who are "the elect lady and her children"?

As to the "elder," this is the title that the author of Third John also uses, and therefore the two letters are most likely from the same hand. He has traditionally been identified with the author of First John, who never gives his name and does not follow the traditional epistolary convention of beginning by referring to the writer and to the addressees. As we shall see, there is much material in Second John that appears also in First John. Furthermore, in the manuscript tradition Second and Third John consistently appear together with First John, and do not seem to have circulated independently. For all these reasons, there is little room to doubt that what we have here are three writings by the same author—although occasionally some scholars have sought to prove otherwise. While "the elder" does not give his name, he has traditionally been called "John." But, as we saw in the Introduction, even if that was his actual name it does not tell us much about who he was, for there is some confusion as to how many early church leaders were called John. Here we shall call him John because this is the name by which he is traditionally known, and because this may have actually been his name. In so doing, we are acknowledging that his writings are part of the Johannine corpus, and have certain affinities with—but also significant differences from—the Gospel of John and the Book of Revelation.

Did John write these three letters in the order in which they now appear? There is no way of knowing. There is so much similarity in content between First and Second John, that it has been argued that Second John is either an earlier letter that John sent and later expanded into First John, or on the contrary, that Second John is a summary of First John. All we can say is that all three Epistles were written at approximately the same time, toward the end of the first century, and that the content of Second John is a much briefer version of First John.

Then there is the question of who are "the elect lady and her children." Some have argued that she is a particular woman, and even that her name was Electa, thus translating the beginning of the Epistle as "The elder to the lady Electa and her children." But most probably the "lady" to whom the elder writes is a church, and her children are its members. There is other ancient Christian literature in which the church is depicted as a matronly woman. This is the case, for instance, in the *Shepherd* of Hermas, where a woman who turns out to be the church guides the author through a series of visions. The view that "the elect lady" is a church seems to be corroborated by the final greeting in the Epistle: "The children of your elect sister send you their greetings." It is highly unlikely that two sisters would be named Electa! Furthermore, by calling her "lady"—*Kyria*—John is giving her the feminine form of the title of Jesus as Lord—*Kyrios*. Thus, to refer to the church as *Kyria* may be an oblique reference to its role as the bride of the

Kyrios. (Although we have capitalized both the masculine and the feminine forms, in ancient Greek writing only capital letters were used, and therefore it is impossible to know what is a proper name or a title and what is not.)

Following traditional epistolary style, John expands what he says about his addressees, declaring that he loves them "in the truth." Although by itself this phrase could simply mean "sincerely," the rest of the sentence makes it clear that John means more than that: it is not only John who thus loves them, "but

> "Jesus said to him, 'I am the way, and the truth, and the life. No one comes to the Father except through me'" (Jn 14:6).

also all who know the truth." In typical Johannine fashion, this "truth" seems to be none other than Jesus Christ, who in the Gospel of John declares himself to be the truth (Jn 14:6), and to whom First John repeatedly refers by that title. This truth—Jesus Christ—"abides in us and will be with us forever." This too is typically Johannine language, for we have already seen that the verb "to abide" appears repeatedly in First John. The truth (which is mentioned five times in the first four verses of Second John) is not a doctrine one holds—although it certainly implies doctrine—but a reality that abides in believers, and in which believers abide.

Then follows a salutation, which is also typical of the epistolary genre (see, for instance, Jude 2; 1 Peter 1:2; 2 Peter 2; Rom. 1:7). Such greetings are often mere formalities, but sometimes do express the particular interests or concerns of the writer. In this specific case, one notes that the rather expected and almost formulaic greeting ends by connecting the greeting itself with two central themes in both the Johannine literature in general and this particular Epistle: "in *truth* and *love*." It is not clear whether this means that Jesus Christ is the Father's Son "in truth and love," or rather—which is more likely—it is the entire congregation that is greeted "in truth and love." But what is clear is that these two—or rather, the unbreakable connection between the two—will be the central theme of the entire Epistle.

In verse 4 the body of the letter begins, making a smooth transition from the customary words of commendation to the actual concern that John wishes to express. There is first the word of commendation: "I was overjoyed to find some of your children walking in the truth." But the very word "some" indicates that not all is well. Apparently John is concerned that not all the children of the "elect lady"—not all the members of the church to which he is writing—are "walking in the truth"—another phrase we have already found in First John.

At this point, we would expect John to bring up the issue of those who are not "walking in the truth," and how it is that they are walking in untruth. But, as he repeatedly does in First John, he connects truth with love by postponing the discussion of truth while he focuses on love.

Apparently those who are not walking in the truth are more than a few, for John addresses the "dear lady"—the church—with an admonition: "let us love one another." This could mean that there were some in that particular congregation who did not love John, or that there were some who did not practice love in the community, or even both, for the John whom we have met in the first Epistle would certainly feel that those who do not love one another do not love him nor the truth in which he invites them to abide. At any rate, as in First John, this call for mutual love is the commandment of love, which is not new, but rather one that his readers have had "from the beginning"—another phrase that we have seen repeatedly in First John. And, as in First John, love is the same as walking in the commandments of God. In short, to obey God is to love, and to walk in the truth is to walk in love.

But what concerns John is not just the manner in which believers relate among themselves. Here again, as in First John, there is a close connection between love and truth, and between lack of love and doctrinal deception. In verse 7, John seems to make an about-face, just as he did in verse 5. Before verse 5, he was speaking of truth. He then shifted in verses 5 and 6 to the subject of love. And now, in verse 7, he returns to the question of truth—now referring to those whom he calls deceivers, the opponents of truth. We have already seen similar shifts in First John. They are not the result of a lack of order or of mental discipline. On the contrary, they seem to be quite purposeful, making it impossible to opt for truth without love, or for love without truth.

The "deceivers" in this Epistle appear to be essentially the same as in First John. They are people "who do not confess that Jesus Christ has come in the flesh." This is exactly what John says in 1 Jn 4:2-3. And here again, as there, he says that these are the antichrist. John's insistence on this matter may surprise us, for today most people who reject what Christianity says about Jesus would say that he was a great man and a teacher, but that he was still just a human being, and any claims as to his divinity are wrong. What we may find surprising is that for the early church the most common problem was not this, but exactly its opposite. The church had to struggle constantly against teachings that denied the true humanity of Jesus, even though they affirmed his divinity or at least his celestial origin. We have already encountered Cerinthus, who is reputed to have opposed the teachings of John in Ephesus. He was one of many who claimed that the physical body of Jesus was just an appearance. This opinion is known as "docetism," from a Greek word that means "to appear" or "to seem." Thus, although not always agreeing among themselves, docetists agreed in rejecting the true humanity of Jesus. This is why John insists so much on the declaration "that Jesus has come in the flesh" as the hallmark of true doctrine. Those who deny this, he would call "deceivers." It is significant to note that this is the same opinion he has of those who do not obey the commandments or do not practice love (1 Jn 2:4).

Most of the rest of the letter, through verse 11, enlarges on this subject. John calls the "elect lady and her children" to be on their guard, lest they lose what they have attained. And then he builds on this by returning to the notion of abiding. By so doing, he builds into the letter a structure much like a sandwich, where "abiding" is the bread (vv. 2, 9) while love and truth—or true doctrine—are the center.

Verses 10 and 11 speak of hospitality. But while most of the New Testament—and the Old—stresses the need to practice hospitality, here John warns the elect lady against being too hospitable. Any who do not hold to the original teaching, that Jesus Christ has come in the flesh, are not to be welcomed. Coming immediately after the references to abiding in the true doctrine, this injunction probably should not be taken literally, as if an actual lady were being told to shut her home to those needing shelter who do not agree with John. More likely, what we have here is a warning to the church not to receive in its midst, as teachers, those whose teachings do not agree with what the church has already received, or anyone who "goes beyond" the teaching of Christ. In other Christian literature of approximately the same time we find that churches were finding it difficult to distinguish among the many itinerant preachers between those who deserved a hearing (and support!) and those who did not. Thus, the *Didache* lists some behaviors and attitudes that distinguish the true prophet from the false. The *Didache*, like John, insists on the consistency between teaching and the practice of love, for one of the marks of the true prophet is asking for support for the needy.[17] Likewise, John sees doctrine as a basic criterion: "those who do not confess that Jesus Christ has come in the flesh" are deceivers and the antichrist. And abiding in truth is juxtaposed to abiding in love, for to walk in the truth—as John would put it—is to love one another.

The letter then ends with an expression of John's desire to visit the "elect lady," and with greetings from "the children of your elect sister"—that is, the members of the church from which John is writing.

The issues raised in this letter are particularly relevant for us today in two ways. First of all, there is the matter of truth and love as two sides of a single coin. In the church today there are some who insist on true doctrine down to the last comma and the last dot. Any who disagree with them in any detail of doctrine are to be rejected as heathen unbelievers. On the other hand, there are those who insist that, since love is the hallmark of Christianity, we should never make judgments as to doctrines or behaviors. Love must be all-encompassing, and this means that no teaching should be declared false, and no conduct should be declared sinful. Over against these two poles, John reminds us that Christian truth cannot exist without love, and Christian love cannot exist without truth. It is not easy to entwine the two. But whenever we find ourselves zealously defending a truth, it may be time to take inventory and make certain we are not lacking in love. And whenever we find ourselves using "love" as an excuse not to proclaim the truth, it may be time to ask ourselves if true love does not demand speaking the truth.

Then, this Epistle is particularly relevant today, when so many versions of the Gospel seem to circulate, and when not all of these are true. Today we have preachers who come to us over radio and television, each with his or her own "ministry," and all asking for our trust and support. Until a few decades ago, major Christian denominations could follow John's advice, of not receiving into their house or welcoming any who did not teach true doctrine. This usually sufficed to protect the believing community from charlatans and others whose teachings were not approved. Today this is more difficult. First of all, there are preachers and teachers asking admission into our living rooms whenever we turn on the television set or listen to the radio, and the organized church has no control over that. Then, there are itinerant preachers who create their own following, going from town to town with their preaching, their songs, and sometimes their claims to healing powers. We cannot reject all of these simply because they do not belong to our denomination, or because a certain board or committee of the denomination has not certified them. What criteria, then, are we to use in such cases? What would be the equivalent today of confessing that Jesus Christ has come in the flesh? What would be the equivalent today of loving all those who abide in the truth? What would be the equivalent today of joining truth and love, and making certain that we abide in both, and that both abide in us?

Chapter 10
A Call to Unity in Love: Third John

If we found it frustrating not to have even the names of "the elder" and the "elect lady" in Second John, our frustration will increase as we realize that in Third John we have quite a wealth of names in just fifteen verses, and still those names tell us little or nothing.

As in Second John, the author remains anonymous, simply using the title of "the elder." We shall continue calling him John, both out of respect for a tradition of long standing and because this may very well have been his name. But the addressee does not remain anonymous. His name is Gaius. Gaius was not a fairly common name in the Roman Empire. Actually, in the New Testament itself there are several references to one Gaius or another. In Romans 16:23, Paul send greetings from "Gaius, who is host to me and to the whole church," and in 1 Corinthians 1:14 he mentions in passing that he baptized Gaius, who apparently is a member of the church in Corinth. In Acts 19:29, Gaius is said to be a Macedonian and one of Paul's traveling companions. Then in Acts 20:4, a certain Gaius is listed again among Paul's companions. But this Gaius is from Derbe, which is not in Macedonia. The problem is that it is impossible to know which of these are the same person, and which are someone else. As to the Gaius to whom John is writing, he may have been one of those mentioned elsewhere in the New Testament, or he may be someone else altogether. As we study the letter, we shall try to glean any other possible information about him. For now, it is clear that John holds him in high esteem. In the first eleven words in the Greek text of the letter, John expresses his love for Gaius three times. In verse 1 he calls him "the *beloved*, whom I *love* in truth." And the very next verse begins by addressing him as "*beloved*."

Then the Epistle gives us two other names. On the negative side there is Diotrephes, whose name is rather uncommon, and about whom no more is known than is said in the Epistle itself. This Diotrephes John criticizes and opposes. We shall try to learn more about why John opposed him as we study the rest of the letter.

On the positive side there is Demetrius. Again, nothing more in known about him than what can be gleaned from this Epistle. Quite possibly his role is much more important than would appear at first. When we read in Paul's letters that he is sending a particular person with a letter, or that he commends someone, we tend to think that this person was little more than a courier or a traveler whom Paul wanted his readers to receive. But most likely what we are reading is what scholars call a "letter of commendation." Such letters had two functions. The first was similar to today's letters of recommendation. We know two people, and we write telling one of them that the other is to be believed, or respected, or admitted into graduate school, or employed. The second function of letters of commendation was just as important—and often even more so. When the author of a letter praised the one who carried it, this was also an indication that the recommended could speak for the sender; that this person knew the sender well enough to explain or interpret the sender's mind. In this second function, ancient letters of commendation were similar to today's "credentials" that an ambassador presents to a foreign government. These credentials indicate that the ambassador is authorized to speak for his or her own government. Likewise, when Paul commends Phoebe (Rom. 16:1-2) or Tychicus (Eph. 6:21; Col. 4:7-8), he is also telling his readers that these people can speak for him, and even have authority to explain anything in his letter that is not clear. This may well be the role of Demetrius in connection with this letter, even though the letter does not spell it out clearly—indeed, it is impossible to tell if Demetrius was already with Gaius, or was the bearer of the letter.

> "I commend to you our sister Phoebe, a deacon of the church at Cenchreae, so that you may welcome her in the Lord as is fitting for the saints, and help her in whatever she may require from you, for she has been a benefactor of many and of myself as well" (Rom. 16:1-2).

What all of this means is that when reading Third John we are in a situation similar to when we suddenly drop into a conversation among people whom we hardly know. It is not difficult for us to have a general idea of what they are talking about; but there are references in the conversation which the participants do not need to explain among themselves, but are not clear to us.

How does this letter relate to the other two attributed to the same author? There are sufficient parallelisms and points of contacts between Second and Third John that one can imagine the two being written at the same time and to the same church. If that is the case, Second John addresses the entire church, while Third John is sent to a particular leading member of that church. In both there is a matter of who is to be welcomed and who is not. Significantly, Second John urges not welcoming those who would deceive the church, while Third John complains about the poor welcome some visitors have received. Thus, one could say that in Third John the shoe is on the other foot. If the two letters are addressed to the same church at the same time, it would follow that in the conflicts within that church

Diotrephes is among those whom John would call "deceivers." The problem is that in Second John it would appear that it is the church whom John is addressing that has the power to welcome or reject others, while in Third John the situation is different, for Diotrephes seems to be a powerful leader who has rejected those whom John would support. Therefore, it would seem reasonable to assume that these two letters, while dealing with similar problems, are written to different communities in slightly different situations, or to a single community at two different times. In Second John, those whom "the elder" would support have the upper hand among "the children of the elect lady." In Third John, they do not—or at least there is a powerful faction led by Diotrephes which John holds to be in error.

As we turn to the first verses of the letter itself, there is much in it that will be familiar from our study of the other two Epistles. Besides the emphasis on love, there is the phrase "love in truth." As already indicated, this may mean simply "love sincerely," or it may mean love in Christ, for in the Epistles "the truth" frequently stands for Christ. Then there is the reference to walking in the truth, which we have encountered repeatedly. And, finally, John refers to those who follow him—or who have come to the faith through him—as "my children."

Using these various images and phrases, verses 2-4 express the writer's concern for Gaius, and his joy at knowing of Gaius' faithfulness. This section of the letter represents the normal epistolary style of the time, in which the information about the writer and the addressee was usually followed by words of appreciation and concern for the latter.

It is in verse 5 that we get to the issue at hand. Apparently some people have been well received by Gaius, and John is commending him for that, and encouraging him to continue along the same path. Who these people were is not exactly clear—again, we are coming in in the middle of an ongoing conversation. John calls them "brothers"—or "brothers and sisters," which the NRSV translates as "friends." But they were "strangers" to Gaius. What Gaius had done for these strangers is not clear. It certainly has something to do with hospitality; but this may mean either providing them shelter and food or receiving them into the congregation as legitimate preachers. Although some commentators call them "emissaries," there is nothing in the letter to suggest that John had sent them. We are told that "they began their journey for the sake of Christ, [literally, 'for the sake of the name'] accepting no support from non-believers." This would seem to imply that they were itinerant preachers. As we have seen, one of the issues the early church had to face was the proliferation of itinerant preachers, and how to determine whose preaching was legitimate and whose was not. In the *Didache*, a document from approximately the same date as the Epistles of John, one of the ways to make this determination is how much support such itinerant preachers expect or request: those who appear to be taking advantage of their ministry are not legitimate, and should not be received as such.[18] Here, John suggests that "accepting no support from non-believers" is a sign of the legitimacy of these preachers. Gaius is encouraged by the affirmation that "we ought to support such people, so that we may become co-workers with the truth."

We are not told how John came to know of what was happening—or had happened—in Gaius' church. Apparently it is through some communication with the itinerant preachers themselves: "They have testified to your love before the church." If the church before which they have testified is where John is, then presumably the preachers are no longer in Gaius' church. In that case, John is not telling Gaius to receive these particular preachers. They have already come and gone, and John is writing after the event. His purpose, rather than to have Gaius receive the preachers, is to commend him for having done so, to condemn Diotrephes for whatever he has done, and to encourage Gaius and strengthen his hand in the continuing conflict within his church.

Diotrephes appears in verse 9. Again, John says nothing about who he is. It is not necessary, for Gaius knows him. According to John, he has already written to that church, apparently in support of the itinerant preachers. But Diotrephes is hungry for power, will not accept John's authority, and has refused to receive the itinerant preachers. Furthermore, Diotrephes has been spreading false charges against John. (The text says "us," which may imply that it is not only John that Diotrephes criticizes, but the entire community that supports him.) We can only surmise what those "false charges" may have been. One possibility is that, as so often happens in such struggles, Diotrephes was accusing John of being hungry for power—just as John was accusing Diotrephes of the same. More likely, however, is the possibility that the "false charges" were accusations that John was teaching false doctrine. In this case, Diotrephes would share the opinions and attitudes of the "deceivers" of Second John and of the "liars" of First John—that is, of those whom he calls "antichrist." However, here the situation is more serious than in Second John, for Diotrephes has apparently taken control of the community and is able not only to refuse hospitality to the itinerant preachers in question, but even to expel from the church those who do offer hospitality.

Verse 11 then returns to Gaius, and to what John expects of him. It summarizes in a few lines much of what we have already seen in the other two Epistles, connecting doing good with knowing—having seen—God.

Then, in verse 12, Demetrius enters the scene. It is not clear whether he is someone who has come to John from Gaius' church or, on the contrary, someone whom John is sending to Gaius and his community. The first part of the verse would point to the first alternative, and the second part of the verse to the second. Most probably, Demetrius has already been in Gaius' church, and has reported to John before returning to that church. He will now serve as John's representative, holding the fort against Diotrephes, until John has the opportunity to come personally. Thus, the entire letter is a commendation of Demetrius as John's representative—which John makes clear: "we also testify for him, and you know that our testimony is true."

Verse 13 is almost identical to Second John 12, and is one of the reasons why some think that Second and Third John were written at the same time, one to the church at large, and the other to John's main supporter there. If so, the words in Second John are a warning against the "deceivers"—including Diotrephes—and those in Third John are intended to encourage Gaius in steadfast opposition to Diotrephes.

Finally, John sends greetings to Gaius from "the friends" where John is, and also to "the friends" where Gaius is. His final words, sending greetings to "each by name," indicate that John was well acquainted with Gaius's community, and that Gaius—and probably others—would know to whom John would send personal greetings.

When read together with Second John, Third John shows the complexity and difficulties that are always inherent in the unavoidable task of "discerning the spirits." In First John 4, the testing of the spirits might seem to be a simple matter of determining who confesses that Jesus has come in the flesh and who does not. But things are not that simple. In all three Epistles, we have seen that belief and action are indissolubly knit together. It would be simple to make a list of doctrines to which all must adhere, and then to declare that any who do not subscribe to all of them are following false spirits and are therefore the antichrists to whom John refers. Actually, even today there are Christian communities that do that. In such lists, many go far beyond John's criterion of confessing that Jesus has come in the flesh, and list such matters as whether the world was created in seven days, or whether "the great tribulation" comes before or after the millennium. Quite often, in the midst of such debates, love suffers, and the church is divided over minor points of doctrine—or even over what in truth are no more than theories or personal opinions. For John, this would not be to "walk in the truth," for true doctrine must lead to love. On the other hand, if we have no criteria for determining who is preaching the truth and who is not, and if "love" means accepting any and all teaching, Christianity dissolves into mush, and is like salt that has lost its flavor. Keeping both truth and love—or even better, knowing that truth without love is false, and that love without truth is not love—is the constant calling to which we must return today.

Notes

1. On this particular theological tradition, and what distinguishes it from others, see Justo L. González, *Christian Thought Revisited: Three Types of Theology*, rev. ed. (Maryknoll, NY: Orbis, 1999).

2. *Journal*, July 18, 1765. Jackson edition, 3:230.

3. Preface to *Sermons on Several Occasions*, Jackson edition, 6:187.

4. Calvin suggests a similar reordering of the words for the sake of clarity: "As the passage is abrupt and involved, that the sense may be made clearer, the words may be thus arranged; 'We announce to you the word of life, which was from the beginning and really testified to us in all manner of ways, that life has been manifested in him;' or, if you prefer, the meaning may be thus given, 'What we announce to you respecting the word of life, has been from the beginning, and *has been openly shewed to us, that life was manifested in him.*'" *Commentary on First John*, 1.1.

5. *Commentary on First John*, 1.

6. *Confessions*, 7.9.14.

7. *The First, Second, and Third Letters of John*, in *The New Interpreter's Bible*, vol 12 (Nashville: Abingdon, 1998), 383.

8. *Didache*, 1-5. Similar words are found in another ancient writing, the *Epistle of Barnabas*, 18-20.

9. Preface to *A Collection of Psalms and Hymns*, 1738. Jackson ed., 14:321.

10. *On the Unity of the Church*, 5.

11. *Commentary on First John*, 2.1.

12. *The Cost of Discipleship* (New York: Macmillan, 1955), 56.

13. Judith M. Lieu, *I, II, & III John: A Commentary, The New Testament Library* (Louisville: Westminster John Knox Press, 2008), 96.

14. *Against Heresies*, 3.3.4.

15. *Ep. To the Smyrneans*, 6. The Ante-Nicene Fathers, 1:179.

16. Lieu, *I, II, & III John*, p. 195.

17. *Didache*, 11.12.

18. *Didache*, 11.9-10.

Suggested Bibliography

Black, C. Clifton, "The First, Second, and Third Letters of John," in *The New Interpreter's Bible*, vol. 12 (Nashville: Abingdon, 1998), 363-469.

Houlden, J. L., *A Commentary on the Johannine Epistles* (New York: Harper & Row, 1973).

Johnson, Earl S., Jr., *James; First and Second Peter; First, Second, and Third John; and Jude*, in *Basic Bible Commentary* (Nashville: Abingdon, 1988).

Lieu, Judith M., *I, II, & III John: A Commentary*, in *The New Testament Library* (Louisville: Westminster John Knox, 2008).

Painter, John, *1, 2, and 3 John*, in *Sacra Pagina Series* (Collegeville: The Liturgical Press, 2002).

Schnackenburg, Rudolf, *The Johannine Epistles: Introduction and Commentary* (New York: Crossroad, 1992).

Smith, D. Moody, *First, Second, and Third John,* in *Interpretation: A Bible Commentary for Teaching and Preaching* (Louisville: John Knox, 1991).

About the Authors

Dr. Justo L. González, a native of Cuba, is a retired professor of historical theology. After completing his PhD in historical theology at Yale University in 1961, he went to Puerto Rico, where he taught at the Evangelical Seminary of Puerto Rico for eight years. He then taught for another eight years at Candler School of Theology. For the last thirty years he has focused on developing programs for the theological education of Hispanics, resulting in the founding of the Asociación par la Educación Teológica Hispana (AETH), the Hispanic Summer Program (HSP), and the Hispanic Theological Initiative (HTI). Jointly, these programs seek to strengthen the Latino leadership in all churches at all levels of education and training. An ordained United Methodist minister, he has also published over a hundred books, mostly in the field of history, but also on various books of Scripture and on theology. His books have been translated into some eight languages. The best known are *The Story of Christianity* (2 vols.) and *A History of Christian Thought* (3 vols.). His next forthcoming book in English is a *Commentary on Luke*, for the series *Belief: A Theological Commentary on the Bible* to be published by Westminster Press in the summer of 2010. Besides his PhD degree from Yale, he has received four honorary doctorates.

Dr. Catherine Gunsalus González, a native of New York, is Professor Emerita of Church History at Columbia Theological Seminary, in Decatur, GA. She completed her PhD in historical theology at Boston University in 1965. She then taught at West Virginia Wesleyan College, where she was also Director of Student Religious Life. In 1970 she began teaching at Louisville Presbyterian Theological Seminary, and in January 1974 she joined the faculty of Columbia Theological Seminary, where she taught until her retirement in 2002. In 1974-75, she was the first woman to preach a series in the widely respected radio program *The Protestant Hour*. She is the author of several books, some jointly with Justo and some on her own. An ordained Presbyterian minister, she has devoted her time to the theological education of women and to the history of liturgy and spirituality. In 2006, the General Assembly of the Presbyterian Church (USA) honored her with its Award for Excellence in Theological Education. Her next forthcoming book is a *Commentary on I and II Peter and Jude*, also for the series *Belief: A Theological Commentary on the Bible*, to be published later in 2010.

Although they travel extensively, Catherine and Justo live in Decatur, GA. They have a daughter, two granddaughters, and two great-grandchildren, all residing also in Georgia. When they are not traveling, writing, or gardening, they enjoy a good mystery story.

Additional Resources

For the Love of God: The Epistles of John Study Guide
Mary Kathryn Pearce
M3089-2010-01 $3.00

Por el Amor de Dios: las Epístolas de Juan
Justo L. y Catherine Gunsalus González
(*For the Love of God: The Epistles of John*, Spanish translation)
M3071-2010-01 $6.50

Por el Amor de Dios: las Epístolas de Juan Guía de Estudio
Diana Lopez
(*For the Love of God: The Epistles of John Study Guide*, Spanish)
M3092-2010-01 $3.00

하나님의 사랑: 요한서신
후스토 L 곤잘레스, 캐서린 건살루스 곤잘레스
Justo L. and Catherine Gunsalus González
(*For the Love of God: The Epistles of John*, Korean)
M3094-2010-01 $6.50

하나님의 사랑: 요한서신 (지침서)
이(홍)혜성

(*For the Love of God: The Epistles of John Study Guide*, Korean)
Hyesung Hong Lee
M3072-2010-01 $3.00

Web site: www.umwmission.org/johnsepistles

Available from: Mission Resource Center, 800-305-9857
www.missionresourcecenter.org